Dedicated

To

All the Past & Present Judges of the Supreme Court of India.

Salute to their wisdom.

Salute to their interpretation of Law.

Salute to their elaborative judgement writing.

TRANSFER OF PROPERTY ACT- SUPREME COURT'S LEADING CASE LAWS

CASE NOTES- FACTS- FINDINGS OF APEX COURT JUDGES & CITATIONS

JAYPRAKASH BANSILAL SOMANI

Contents

Contents

Preface

Dear Learned Advocates of the Trial Courts, Session Courts, Tribunals, High Courts, Supreme Court, Corporates & Individuals

I am very delighted to provide you a book on 'TRANSFER OF PROPERTY ACT'- Supreme Court of India's Leading Case Laws'.

In this book you will get...

1. Name of the Case i. e. Cause title

2.Relevant Sections discussed in the case

3. Hon'ble Judges/Coram of the case

4.Number of PDF Pages in Original Judgement of the case

5. All available Citations of the case

6. Case Note with appeal allowed/ dismissed or disposed off

7. Facts of the case

8. Hon'ble Apex Court's findings, while dismissing/allowing or disposing the appeal

9. Ratio Decidendi if any.

My special thanks to Manupatra, because of their web portal I can compile this book in well manner. I am also thankful to Notion Press to support me to publish & market this book throughout the Country. Thanks to my Juniors, Advocate Colleagues & Insolvency Professional Colleagues to support me in this venture.

Mr Rachit Manchanda has helped me a lot to compile this book.

I hope this book will add some value addition in the wealth of your legal knowledge. Your positive feedbacks will boost me to compile/ write further books & negative feedbacks will improve my skills. Kindly send your valuable feedbacks by email.

Thanks with Regards,

Jayprakash B. Somani

Advocate, Supreme Court of India

Email: jaysomani64@gmail.com

Web Site:www.jayprakashsomani.com

Call: 8384051134, 9322188701, 9318381287

• • •

Acknowledgements

Printed & Published by
Notion Press
No. 8, 3rd Cross Street,
CIT Colony, Mylapore,
Chennai, Tamil Nadu- 600004

• • •

Managed by
Jayprakash Somani Advocates & Solicitors
Law Firm for Supreme Court of India
Delhi Office
257 C, Pocket 1, Mayur Vihar Phase 1, Delhi 110091.
Call 8384051134, 9322188701, 8459194576, 9318381287
01141051516
Supreme Court Chamber
312, 3rd Floor, M. C. Setalvad Block, In front of 'D' Gate, Bhagwan Das Road, Supreme Court of India, New Delhi 110001
Contact: 8459194576, 9811011747,
www.jayprakashsomani.com

• • •

Books are available online at
1. Notion Press: https://notionpress.com/author/jayprakash_somani
2. Amazon: https://www.amazon.in/s?k=jayprakash+somani
3. Flipkart: https://www.flipkart.com/search?q=Jayprakash%20Somani

• • •

CHAPTER I

The State of Kerala and Ors. Vs. Joseph & Company, 2021

Hon'ble Judges/Coram: Hemant Gupta and A.S. Bopanna, JJ.

Relevant Section:

Transfer Of Property Act, 1882 - Section 111; Section 112

Equivalent Citation: AIR2021SC4486, 2021(5)ALD271, 2021(6)ALT1, 2021 (3) CCC 544 , 2021(6)KLT120, (2021)7MLJ341, 2021(4)RCR(Civil)180 MANU/SC/0598/2021

No. of page is the original judgement: 7

Case Note:

Property - Breach of Lease Terms - Termination of lease - Sections 111, 112 of the Transfer of Property Act, 1882 - Transfers made in violation of lease terms - Land in question leased by the government - Competent authority issued notice upon breach of lease - Rent in the meantime paid continuously to lessor - Whether in such circumstances lease in question validly terminated?

Brief Facts of the case:

The present matter arose from transfer of portion of land originally held by erstwhile Travancore-Cochin Government. Vide notification in the year 1953 certain abandoned portion of the land was auctioned. Dispute sprung from subsequent transfers and rectification application moved in between but was put into abeyance. The terms of lease on which transfer was made was alleged to be breached causing issuance of notice. Appellant assailed the order disposing petition to the extent of quashing the order declining value of usufructs (Ex. 41). The order (Ex. 39) terminating lease in favour of Respondent was upheld. Division Bench of the High Court through the impugned order allowed the appeal filed Respondent and thereby setting aside the order terminating lease and the appeal filed by State of Kerala was dismissed. Hence, the present appeal.

The genesis of the case is that erstwhile Travancore-Cochin Government had by a notification in the year 1953 auctioned certain abandoned portions of Beatrice estate. One Mr. P.I. Joseph-responded to the said notification and offered his bid to an extent of 246.26 acres out of the South Block and took possession on 10.05.1955. However, no lease agreement was entered into between him and the government. In the meanwhile, the said Mr. P.I. Joseph assigned the said property in favour of Mr. K.K. Joseph. Pursuant to such transaction dated 28.02.1974 between Mr. P.I. Joseph and Mr. K.K. Joseph, the Government of Kerala, executed a lease deed dated 15.12.1979 in favour of Mr. K.K. Joseph. Though the lease deed was executed in favour of Mr. K.K. Joseph, it is contended by the lessee that Mr. K.K. Joseph was representing the partnership firm registered in the name and style M/s. Joseph & Company, of which he was the Managing Partner.

Held,

When there was breach providing the right to terminate the lease in respect of the entire leased land, even if the lease rental paid by the lessee has been accepted by the Appellant-lessor, it has not been shown that the requirement of the conditions in the proviso to Section 112 of the T.P. Act is satisfied. In the present situation, the land is leased by the government and when the breach had occurred the competent authority had issued the notice and the proceedings was initiated. Once the proceedings had been initiated even if the lease rental was received the same is saved under the second proviso. Further the situation is also that the payment of the rental made to the government would in any event be accepted as different functions are performed by different offices and any amount tendered will be received. That cannot give any advantage to the lessee merely because the rent has been tendered in the government office and the same has been innocuously accepted without there being specific reference to waiver.

A perusal of the extracted portion from the sale deed dated 16.12.1983 would indicate the outright nature of sale of a portion of the leased land. It is sold for a sale consideration despite knowing that the property belonging to the government is granted under lease. The document itself would indicate the intention of the parties and also the fact that possession was parted without consent of the lessor which was a clear breach of Clause 14 in the lease deed.

When public largesse is bestowed on certain terms and conditions, a term of the lease deed is to be strictly adhered to and when Clause 14 provides that the lessee shall not be entitled to sublet or assign his interest in the lease except with the previous permission in writing of the lessor, it does not matter as to whether the breach committed is by assigning a portion of the leased land or the whole when such interest of the lessee has been transferred without previous permission of the lessor. In the instant case, despite being a lessee the Respondent has executed an absolute sale deed in respect of the leased land which belongs to the government and such breach cannot be condoned.

• • •

CHAPTER II

K. Raheja Development Corporation Vs. State of Karnataka, 2005

Hon'ble Judges/Coram: S.N. Variava and A.R. Lakshmanan, JJ.

Relevant Section:

Transfer Of Property Act, 1882 - Section 53A, Karnataka Sales Tax Act, 1957 - Section 2(1) Section 2(1)(k)(viii), Section 2(1)(u1), Section 2(1)(v-i), Section 5, Section 5B;

Equivalent Citation: 2005(32)AIC455, AIR2005SC2350, 2005(5)ALT24(SC), JT2005(5)SC161, 2005(2)KLT822(SC), (2005)3MLJ151(SC), (2005)5SCC162, [2005]3SCR1210, [2005]141STC298(SC), 2006[3]S.T.R.337(S.C.), MANU/SC/0357/2005

No. of page is the original judgement: 5

Case Note:

Sales Tax - Assessment - Karnataka Sales Tax Act - Section 2(1) - Appellant builders constructs residential apartment after entering into agreement with owners of land - Assessment authority passed assessment order claiming tax on appeal to Additional Joint Commissioner of Commercial Taxes (Appeal) it was held that tax was payable as there was transfer of property in goods pursuant to a works contract - Appeal to Karnataka High Court - Dismissed - Appeal assailing propriety - Whether the Appellants are dealers and are liable to pay turnover tax under the Karnataka Sales Tax Act - Held, `works contract' has an inclusive definition - Includes "any agreement" for carrying out building or construction activity for cash, deferred payment or other valuable consideration - Hence, appellants are owners to the extent that they have entered into agreements to carry out construction activity on behalf of somebody else for cash, deferred payment or other valuable consideration - They would be carrying out a works contract and would become liable to pay turnover tax on the transfer of property in the goods involved in such works contract - Appeal dismissed.

Brief facts of the case:

The Appellants carry on the business of real estate development and allied contracts. They are having their Office at Bangalore. They enter into development Agreements with owners of lands. Thereafter they get plans sanctioned. After approval of the plans they construct residential apartments and/or commercial complexes. In most cases before they construct the residential apartments and/or commercial complexes they enter into Agreements of Sale with intended purchasers. The Agreements would provide that on completion of the construction the residential apartments or the commercial complex would be handed over to the purchasers who would get an undivided interest in the land also. The owners of the land would then transfer the ownership directly to the society which is being formed under the Karnataka Ownership Flats (Regulation of Promotion of Construction, Sales, Management and Transfer) Act, 1974.

The question which arises for consideration is whether the Appellants are dealers and are liable to pay turnover tax under the Karnataka Sales Tax Act.

The Appellants filed returns showing Nil liability to pay tax on the footing that there was no transfer of any property in goods either by itself or by virtue of any works contract. The Adjudicating Authority did not accept their contention and passed an Assessment Order claiming tax.

Against the Assessment Order, the Appellants went in Appeal to the Additional Joint Commissioner of Commercial Taxes (Appeal). The Additional Joint Commissioner held that tax was payable as there was transfer of property in goods pursuant to a works contract.

Held,

If the Prospective Purchaser commits default in payment of any of the installments of consideration aforesaid on their respective due dates (time being the essence of the contract) and/or in observing and performing any of the terms and conditions of this Agreement, the Holders/Developers shall be at liberty, after giving 15 days notice specifying the breach and if the same remains not rectified within that time, to terminate this Agreement, in which event, a sum equivalent to 10% of the amounts that may till then have been paid by the Prospective Purchaser to the Holders and the Developers respectively shall stand forfeited. The Holders and the Developers shall, however, on such termination, refund to the Prospective Purchaser the balance amounts of the installments of part payment, if any, which may have till then been paid by the Prospective Purchaser to the Holders and the Developers respectively but without any further amount by way of interest or otherwise. On the Holder/Developers terminating this Agreement under this Clause, they shall be at liberty to dispose off the said Unit/s and the said fractional interest in the land to any other person as they deem fit, at such price as they may determine and the Prospective Purchaser shall not be entitled to question such sale, disposal or to claim any amount from them."

Thus the Appellants are undertaking to build as developers for the prospective purchaser. Such construction/development is to be on payment of a price in various installments set out in the Agreement. As the Appellants are not the owners they claim a "lien" on the property. Of course, under clause 7 they have right to terminate the Agreement and to dispose off the unit if a breach is committed by the purchaser. However, merely having such a clause does not mean that the agreement ceases to be a works contract within the meaning of the term in the said Act. All that this means is that if there is a termination and that particular unit is not resold but retained by the Appellants, there would be no works contract to that extent. But so long as there is no termination the construction is for and on behalf of purchaser. Therefore, it remains a works contract within the meaning of the term as defined under the said Act. It must be clarified that if the agreement is entered into after the flat or unit is already constructed, then there would be no works contract. But so long as the agreement is entered into before the construction is complete it would be a works contract.

In this view of the matter, the Judgment of the High Court to the extent that it confirms with the above-mentioned view stands confirmed. We do not approve the observations in *Mittal Investment Corporation's* case (supra) which are contrary to the view expressed above. As on the main aspects we agree with the High Court Judgment, we see no reason to interfere.

The Appeal stands dismissed. There will be no order as to costs

• • •

CHAPTER III

Vithaldas Jagannath Khatri (D) through Shakuntala and Ors. Vs. The State of Maharashtra Revenue and Forest Department and Ors., 2019

Hon'ble Judges/Coram: Sanjay Kishan Kaul and K.M. Joseph, JJ.

Relevant Section:

Maharashtra Agricultural Lands (Ceiling On Holdings) Act 1961 - Section 18; Section 11; Section 4; Transfer Of Property Act, 1882 - Section 122; Section 123

Equivalent Citation: 2019(11)SCALE704, (2020)16SCC25, MANU/SC/1188/2019

No. of page is the original judgement: 32

Case Note:

Family - Partition deed - Transfer of the interest - Sections 11 and 12 of Maharashtra Agricultural Lands (Ceiling on Holdings) Act, 1961 - Issue involved in present case was relating to legality of partition deed executed on dated 31st January, 1970 - Whether land allotted to daughters was to be excluded from account of family unit of Shri Vithaldas in determining surplus land under Act, 1961 Facts: Present Court is concerned with the Act, 1961. The said Act also went through many amendments, most importantly the aspect of plugging loopholes, whereby owners having land in excess of the ceiling limit would endeavour to somehow re-distribute it among the family to bring it within the ceiling limit, or at least, to reduce the excess land. In present case, Court is concerned with one document, which is the Partition Deed dated 31st January, 1970, which has been duly registered, i.e., both the document and its registration are undisputedly before the cut-off date of 26.9.1970. The Partition deed has been executed between five parties-late Shri Vithaldas Jagannath Khatri and his then minor son and three minor daughters. Two of the minor daughters attained majority before the commencement date of 2.10.1975, though they were not major on 26.9.1970. In terms of this document, the agricultural land of the Hindu Undivided Family ('HUF') is sought to be divided by mentioning all the parties as part of the HUF. The lands were stated to be used jointly and shares in the lands were given to both, the minor son and the daughters. An intra-court appeal was preferred, which was dismissed vide impugned order. The Division Bench agreed with the findings that, the partition effected vide Partition Deed dated 31.1.1970 was unnatural as it alienated properties to minor daughters, and that a female child could not get a share in the ancestral property, even though it was effected before the relevant date of 26.9.1970. Once again, as reflected in the records, the factum of cultivation of land by late Vithaldas was taken into account. The attainment of the age of majority by the elder two daughters, before the commencement date, 2.10.1975, was also ignored as irrelevant. The Appellants before the Division Bench also sought to raise the issue of the two elder daughters not being arrayed as parties in the cross-objections, even though their existing rights were being affected. Further, it was argued that none of the members of the HUF had assailed the Partition Deed on any account. These pleas also did not find favour on the ground that, it was late Vithaldas who sought to lose the land and, in effect, it was for him to see how to confer the rights on his two elder daughters. The two elder daughters were held to form part of the family unit. Special Leave Petition ('SLP') was filed only by late Vithaldas, through his legal representatives. The two elder daughters are, thus, Appellants as legal heirs of late Vithaldas, in the present proceedings. This is of significance as the contention of Respondents is that the two elder daughters only stepped into the shoes of late Vithaldas, and that they cannot de novo start proceedings in their own rights. Held, while referring matter to a Larger Bench 1. Section 11 specifically talks about the partition deed in a similar manner and, thus, not only transfers whether by way of sale, gift, mortgage with possession, exchange, lease, assignment of land for maintenance, surrender of a tenancy or resumption of land by a landlord or any other disposition, are included, even the avenue by way of a partition deed has been shut out, unless it has been executed prior to the cut-off date. There is no doubt that in the present case, the partition deed was executed before the cut-off date of 26.9.1970 and registered even prior to that date.

Brief facts of the case:

Family - Partition deed - Transfer of the interest - Sections 11 and 12 of Maharashtra Agricultural Lands (Ceiling on Holdings) Act, 1961 - Issue involved in present case was relating to legality of partition deed executed on dated 31st January, 1970 - Whether land allotted to daughters was to be excluded from account of family unit of Shri Vithaldas in determining surplus land under Act, 1961 Facts: Present Court is concerned with the Act, 1961. The said Act also went through many amendments, most importantly the aspect of plugging loopholes, whereby owners having land in excess of the ceiling limit would endeavour to somehow re-distribute it among the family to bring it within the ceiling limit, or at least, to reduce the excess land. In present case, Court is concerned with one document, which is the Partition Deed dated 31st January, 1970, which has been duly registered, i.e., both the document and its registration are undisputedly before the cut-off date of 26.9.1970. The Partition deed has been executed between five parties-late Shri Vithaldas Jagannath Khatri and his then minor son and three minor daughters. Two of the minor daughters attained majority before the commencement date of 2.10.1975, though they were not major on 26.9.1970. In terms of this document, the agricultural land of the Hindu Undivided Family ('HUF') is sought to be divided by mentioning all the parties as part of the HUF. The lands were stated to be used jointly and shares in the lands were given to both, the minor son and the daughters. An intra-court appeal was preferred, which was dismissed vide impugned order. The Division Bench agreed with the findings that, the partition effected vide Partition Deed dated 31.1.1970 was unnatural as it alienated properties to minor daughters, and that a female child could not get a share in the ancestral property, even though it was effected before the relevant date of 26.9.1970. Once again, as reflected in the records, the factum of cultivation of land by late Vithaldas was taken into account. The attainment of the age of majority by the elder two daughters, before the commencement date, 2.10.1975, was also ignored as irrelevant. The Appellants before the Division Bench also sought to raise the issue of the two elder daughters not being arrayed as parties in the cross-objections, even though their existing rights were being affected. Further, it was argued that none of the members of the HUF had assailed the Partition Deed on any account. These pleas also did not find favour on the ground that, it was late Vithaldas who sought to lose the land and, in effect, it was for him to see how to confer the rights on his two elder daughters. The two elder daughters were held to form part of the family unit. Special Leave Petition ('SLP') was filed only by late Vithaldas, through his legal representatives. The two elder daughters are, thus, Appellants as legal heirs of late Vithaldas, in the present proceedings. This is of significance as the contention of Respondents is that the two elder daughters only stepped into the shoes of late Vithaldas, and that they cannot de novo start proceedings in their own rights. Held, while referring matter to a Larger Bench 1. Section 11 specifically talks about the partition deed in a similar manner and, thus, not only transfers whether by way of sale, gift, mortgage with possession, exchange, lease, assignment of land for maintenance, surrender of a tenancy or resumption of land by a landlord or any other disposition, are included, even the avenue by way of a partition deed has been shut out, unless it has been executed prior to the cut-off date. There is no doubt that in the present case, the partition deed was executed before the cut-off date of 26.9.1970 and registered even prior to that date.

2. This Court, in Uttar Chand v. State of Maharashtra, while dealing with the very statute has opined that the cut-off date would be sacrosanct. The factual contours dealt with partition before the cut-off date, as also sale of land. Once the cut-off date is provided, it was observed that they fell completely outside the ambit of the provisions of the Act and, thus, the High Court would not be justified in presuming that the transfers made were either collusive or fraudulent.

3. The order passed by the competent authority, being the SDO, insofar as the two elder daughters are concerned, held in their favour as far as the lands vested in them, in pursuance of the Partition Deed. There was, thus, no occasion for them to file an appeal, nor did they so file an appeal. Other members of the family, who filed the appeal, did not implead them as parties. Once again, naturally so, as they would not be the interested parties, or even pro forma parties in that behalf. However, once the State decided to file cross-objections and, in that, impugned even that portion of the order of the SDO which held in favour of the two elder daughters, there is no hesitation in stating that, they were necessary parties to those proceedings. It is no answer to say that since the effect of the land ceiling would be to restrict the area of their father, late Vithaldas, it is for Vithaldas to see how he can benefit his daughters. This fundamental defect cannot be cured in the subsequent proceedings, as the right of appeal is a statutory right and an important one.

Held,

It is true that this is a case where as regards the elder daughters, they were not parties in the appeal in which the cross-objection was filed.

Also, no doubt the elder daughters and others were Respondents in the Writ Petition and Letter Patent Appeal. It may be true that a Respondent and even a person who is not a party can with leave prefer an appeal. But when they have not challenged the order of the Tribunal and even the judgment of the learned Single Judge and as the Vithaldas had fully contested the matter and in view of my finding that the properties allotted to the elder daughters, are liable to be found held by Vithaldas, I would not be inclined to interfere, particularly, as I have noted above when the perusal of the Special Leave Petition would reveal that Vithaldas (now deceased) through the LRs-the Petitioners is shown in the cause title. It must be remembered that the Petitioners upon the passing away of Vithaldas during the pendency of the Latter Patent Appeal were recorded as his legal representatives.

I would also, at any rate, in this regard, in this case invoke the principles laid down in Taherakhatoon (D) By L.Rs. v. Salambin Mohammad MANU/SC/0139/1999 : 1999 (2) SCC 635 and refuse to interfere.

I would think, therefore, the appeal must fail and it stands dismissed.

In view of difference of opinions and the distinguishing judgments (Hon'ble Sanjay Kishan Kaul, J. allowed the appeal and Hon'ble K.M. Joseph, J. dismissed the appeal), the matter be placed before Hon'ble the Chief Justice of India for referring the matter to a Larger Bench.

• • •

CHAPTER IV

Vasantkumar Radhakisan Vora Vs. The Board of Trustees of the Port of Bombay, 1990

Hon'ble Judges/Coram: K.N. Saikia and K. Ramaswamy, JJ.

Relevant Sections:

Transfer Of Property Act, 1882 - Section 106, Section 109, Section 111(h), Section 2(d), Section 23(1)(b), Section 5, Section 57, Constitution Of India - Article 136, Article 14, Article 15(4), Article 16(4), Article 226, Article 227; General Clauses Act 1897 - Section 17, Section 6; Land Acquisition Act, 1894 [repealed] - Section 11; Major Port Trusts Act, 1963 - Section 133, Section 133(2A), Section 133(2A)(C), Section 17(1), Section 29(1), Section 29(1)(b), Section 43; Presidency Small Cause Courts Act, 1882 - Section 41, Section 45, Section 46, Section 47, Section 46(2), Section 49;

Equivalent Citation: AIR1991SC14, JT1990(3)SC609, 1990(2)SCALE297, (1991)1SCC761, [1990]3SCR825, MANU/SC/0005/1991

No. of page is the original judgement: 8

Case Note:

Property - estoppel - Sections 106, 109 and 111 of Transfer of Property Act, 1882, Section 26 of Bombay Port Trust Act, 1879 and Section 133 of Major Port Trust Act, 1963 - respondent statutory body corporate constituted under Section 26 having power to acquire and hold movable and immovable property and to lease or to sell that property - one such property was leased to appellant - he was served with notice under Section 106, terminating tenancy and to deliver possession within one month - meanwhile Major Port trust Act made applicable - appellant contended that with passing of this Act, State Act ceased to be operative and quit notice issued under Section 106 became ineffective - also pleaded that respondent promised to give on lease portion of building on payment of certain amount - amount paid by appellant - he alleged that respondent is estopped by promissory estoppel to eject tenant - there can be no promissory estoppel against legislature in exercise of its legislative functions nor can Government of public authority be debarred from enforcing statutory prohibition - appellant liable to be ejected.

Brief facts of the case:

The respondent is a statutory body corporate initially constituted under the Bombay Port Trust Act, 1879 (Bombay Act 6 of 1879), for short 'State Act'. Under Section 26 thereof, the Board has power to acquire and hold movable and immovable property and also has power to lease, to sell or otherwise convey movable and immovable property which may have become vested in or acquired by them. The respondent has appointed A.J. Mescarnas, Assistant Estate Manager as their power of attorney holder to lease Out its properties from time to time or terminate the leases and to lay action for ejectment, etc. The respondent owns the Building bearing Old R.R. No. 941 known as 'Frere Land Estate" in which room No. 2 admeasuring 28.27 sq. meters was leased out to Vasantkumar Radhakisan Vora, for short 'Vasantkumar'. The appellants are his legal representatives. He was served with a notice under Section 106 read with Section 111(h) of the Transfer of Property Act terminating the tenancy in terms of the covenants of lease and was asked to deliver possession of the demised property giving one month's time from 22nd January, 1975.

It was served on Vasantkumar on January 28, 1975. The notice of termination thereby became effective from 28th February, 1975. In the meanwhile Major Port Trust Act, 1963 (Act No. 38 of 1963), for short the "Central Act", was made applicable to the Bombay Port Trust by operation of Section 133(2A) with effect from February 1, 1975. After the expiry of one month, ejectment application was filed under Section 41 of the Bombay Presidency Small Cause Courts Act (Act 15 of 1882) as amended under 1963 Maharashtra Amendment Act, against Vasantkumar and another for delivery of possession. After 1976 Amendment Act 19 of 1976 came into force suits were laid against three other tenants. It was pleaded by the respondent that it is a successor in interest of the Board under the State Act and were entitled to eject the tenants and to the possession of the demised portions. The plea of Vasantkumar in his written statement elaborated by the learned Counsel, is that the suit is not maintainable. Since the State Act ceased to be operative with effect from February 1, 1975, the quit notice issued under Section 106 read with Section 111(h) of Transfer of Property Act became ineffective and without determining the tenancy afresh, the suit was not validly laid. It was also pleaded that the respondent had promised that in deposit of certain amount which the tenant did, Vasantkumar would be given on lease of a portion in the reconstructed building. Thereby the respondent is estopped by promissory estoppel to have the tenant ejected.

It may be mentioned at this juncture that one suit was dismissed on the ground that the tenancy was not duly determined as per law. Other suits were decreed. No appellate forum has been prescribed under Amendment Act of 1963 but a substantive suit on original side provided was available. By Maharashtra Amendment Act 19 of 1976 to the principal Act such a right to appeal was incorporated. Vasantkumar filed writ petition in the High Court under Articles 226 and 227 and others filed regular appeals to a Bench of two Judges of the Small Cause Court and are stated to be pending.

Held,

Sri Tunara further submitted that the tenant did not derive title, namely, lease-hold right from the respondent Port Trust under the Central Act. That the tenant disputed the title and it is a sufficient defence under the explanation to Section 43 to non suit the respondent in the summary proceeding. It was open to the respondent to file a regular suit. The Small Cause Court ought to have rejected the application on that ground and the High Court would have gone into the question. It being a pure question of law, this Court may permit the appellant to argue on the point for the first time in this Court. It is undoubtedly true as held by catena of decisions of this Court that a pure question of law, untramelled by questions of fact, which goes to the roots of the jurisdiction, could be permitted to be raised for the first time in an appeal under Article 136 of the Constitution. We are afraid, we cannot permit the appellant to raise this point for the following reasons:

Firstly, except making a bald averment in the written statement that the "suit is not maintainable" nothing has been pleaded in detail in the written statement- Admittedly this point was neither taken in the writ petition nor argued in the High Court. It is not even raised in the grounds, of appeal in this Court nor even in points raised in the synopsis of the case. It is stated that remotely it was raised in the rejoinder. Since it is a mixed question of facts and law and not being a pure question of law, we cannot permit to raise the point for the first time, that too, when it would prejudice the respondent of their case at this stage. We accordingly decline to go into the question. We would also straighten the record and state that the appellants raised in the writ petition the vires of Sections 2, 3 and 4 of the Maharashtra Amending Act, 1963 introducing Section 42(A) in Chapter VII of the Presidency Small Cause Courts Act and deleting Sections 45 to 47 from the Principal Act and of an amended Section 49 thereof as well as Sec, 46(2) of the Presidency Small Cause Courts Act 3S amended by Maharashtra Amendment Act of 1976 as offending Article 14 of the Constitution, and unsuccessfully argued before the Division Bench of the High Court same point was raised in the grounds of appeal in this Court. Though the appeal was argued for three days, Mr. Tunara did not argue this point across the Bar, nor we had the advantage of hearing the learned Solicitor General. Even in a written brief running into 44 pages submitted by the counsel, he did not deal with this point. The counsel, after arguing the two points dealt with earlier, has devoted his time oil the question of jurisdiction of the trial court under Section 41, despite our repeatedly reminding him that this point was neither raised, nor argued in the High Court. At the end he stated that he had elaborately argued the point of vires before the Single Judge and the Division Bench and except repetition of the same once over, he could do no better by further arguing here. Therefore, this Court could go through the judgment and deal with the point. We deprecate this practice, When a constitutional question has been raised and does arise for consideration, unless there is a full-dressed argument addressed by either side before this Court no satisfactory resolution could be made. Mere paraphrasing the judgment of the High Court in particular when it relates to the local laws is no proper decision making Therefore, after giving our anxious consideration, we, with great anguish, decline to go into the point. Except these, no other points have been Accordingly we do not find any merit in the appeal.

The appeal is dismissed, but in the circumstances without costs.

• • •

CHAPTER V

Sonia Bhatia Vs. State of U.P. and Ors., 1981

Hon'ble Judges/Coram: A. Vardarajan, S. Murtaza Fazal Ali and V. Balakrishna Eradi, JJ.

Relevant Section:

Transfer Of Property Act, 1882 - Section 122

Equivalent Citation: AIR1981SC1274, 1981 (7) ALR 244, 1981(1)SCALE491, (1981)2SCC585, [1981]3SCR239, 1981(13)UJ521, MANU/SC/0363/1981

No. of page is the original judgement: 8

Case Note:

Property - benami transaction - whether on basis of gift can property transfer when Act come into force - Act passed in year 1960 and in 1972 grand father of appellant executed gift deed transferring title of 80 bighas land - taking away land from large tenure holders and distributing with landless persons - Act does not allow inheritance of property through gift deed - by this process few individual may suffer severe hardship but it cannot be defence - property of appellant rightly taken over by respondent - appellant not liable for inheritance of property under gift.

Brief facts of the case:

This appeal by special leave is directed against a judgment dated December 21, 1978 of the Allahabad High Court allowing the writ petition filed by the State of U.P. before the Court.

The case arose out of an order passed by the Prescribed Authority under the U.P. Imposition of Ceiling on Land Holdings Act, 1960 (hereinafter referred to as the 'Act'), as amended up to date, by which the said Authority rejected the claim of the petitioners on the basis of a gift which had been executed by her grandfather by a registered document dated January 28, 1972. The Act was passed as far back as 1960 but by virtue of an amendment, being U.P. Act. No. 18 of 1973, Section 5 was introduced which placed a ceiling on any tenure holder to hold land in excess of the ceiling area fixed under the Act. Section 5 contained various Sub-sections but in the instant case we are concerned only with Sub-section (6) as also Clause (b) of the proviso to the said Sub-section. By another amendment, being U.P. Act No. 2 of 1975, which was given retrospective operation with effect from

8.6.1973 Explanation I, alongwith its Sub-clauses, was added to Sub-section (6) of Section 5.

The decision in the present case turns upon the interpretation of Sub-section (6) of Section 5 and the proviso therein in order to determine the validity of the deed of gift said to have been executed by Chunni Lal Bhatiya, the grandfather of the petitioner Sonia and respondent No. 4 before the District Judge.

To begin with, we might like to state here that the facts of the case undoubtedly reveal that if the provisions of the said Sub-section (6) were to apply it would work serious hardship to the petitioner but as we are concerned with interpretation of an important statute the mere fact that a correct interpretation may lead to hardship would not be a valid consideration for distorting the language of the statutory provisions.

Held,

We fully endorse the observations made by the Division Bench which lay down the correct law on the subject and we overrule the decision of Banerji, J. in Fateh Singh's case (supra).

28. Lastly, it was urged by Mr. Kacker that this is an extremely hard case where the grand-father of the donee wanted to make a beneficial provision for his grand-daughter after having lost his two sons in the prime of their life due to air crash accidents while serving in the Air Force. It is true that the District Judge has come to a clear finding that the gift in question is bona fide and has been executed in good faith but as the gift does not fulfil the other ingredients of the section, namely, that it is not for adequate consideration, we are afraid, however laudable the object of the donor may have been, the gift has to fail because the genuine attempt of the donor to benefit his granddaughter seems to have been thwarted by the intervention of Sub-section (6) of Section 5 of the Act. This is undoubtedly a serious hardship but it cannot be helped. We must remember that the Act is a valuable piece of social legislation with the avowed object of ensuring equitable distribution of the land by taking away land from large tenure holders and distributing the same among landless tenants or using the same for public utility schemes which is in the larger interest of the community at large.

The Act seems to implement one of the most important constitutional directives contained in Part IV of the Constitution of India. If in this process a few individuals suffer severe hardship that cannot be helped, for individual interests must yield to the larger interests of the community or the country as indeed every noble cause claims its martyr.

As this was the only point raised before us, we find no merit in the same.

For the reasons given above, we hold that the High Court was right in allowing the writ petition in respect of the gift in question. The appeal fails and is accordingly dismissed but without any order as to costs.

• • •

CHAPTER VI

Raptakos Brett & Co. Vs. Ganesh Property, 1998

Hon'ble Judges/Coram: S.B. Majmudar and M. Jagannadha Rao, JJ.

Relevant Sections:

Transfer of Property Act, 1882 - Section 4, Section 5(1), Section 111(a), Section 108, Section 108(q), Section 116, Section 111; Indian Partnership Act, 1932 - Section 56, Section 57, Section 58, Section 59, Section 69, Section 69(2), Section 69(3); West Bengal Rent Act; Indian Arbitration Act, 1940 - Section 8(2); Karnataka Cinemas (Regulation) Act, 1964; Rule 6; Indian Railways Act, 1989 - Section 77; Indian Contract Act, 1972; Section 1; Limitation Act - Section 14; Companies Act, 1913 - Section 171; Code of Civil Procedure, 1908 (CPC) - Section 80; Order 7 Rule 11, Order 7 Rule 11(d), Order 7 Rule 13, Order 23 Rule 1(3), Order 40 Rule 1; Rent Restriction Act

Equivalent Citation: 1998(2)ARC710, 1998 (4) CCC 1, MANU/SC/2253/1998

No. of page is the original judgement: 14

Case Note:

Civil - Suit for possession and damages for illegal occupation - Whether the suit filed by the Respondent was barred under Section 69(2) of the Partnership Act either wholly or in part and if the suit was so barred, whether subsequent registration of the Plaintiff's firm under the Partnership Act could revive the suit to make it competent at least from the date on which such registration pending the suit was obtained by the Respondent firm?

Brief Facts of the case:

The Respondent-Plaintiff was the owner of suit premises. The said premises was rented to the Appellant-Defendant on a monthly rent by a registered lease for a period of 21 years. On the expiry of the said period, the Respondent-Plaintiff alleging to be a registered partnership firm, filed the aforesaid suit praying for a decree for possession as well as damages for illegal occupation of the premises by the Appellant-Defendant. The defence of the Appellant-Defendant was that after the expiry of the lease period, it had continued to be a tenant by acceptance of rent by the Defendant-landlord and hence it had become a tenant by holding over Under Section 116 of the Transfer of Property Act, 1882 (Property Act). Further defence was taken by the Appellant-Defendant by way of a separate application seeking dismissal of the suit under Order VII, Rule 11(d) of Code of Civil Procedure (CPC) on the ground that the suit for possession as filed by the Plaintiff-Respondent, which was an unregistered partnership firm, was not maintainable

Learned trial Judge framed relevant issues on the pleading and came to the conclusion that the Defendant-Appellant was not a tenant holding over and was in unlawful possession of the premises after the expiry of the lease period. On the question of maintainability of the suit, the trial Court held that the suit was not hit by Section 69, Sub-section (2) of the Indian Partnership Act, 1932 (for short the Partnership Act'). Accordingly, a decree for possession was passed. The Appellant-Defendant carried the matter in first appeal before the High court. As noted earlier, the learned Single Judge who decided the said appeal, held against the Appellant-Defendant and dismissed the appeal. That is how the Appellant-Defendant is before us in the present case.

Held,

On the expiry of the period of lease, the erstwhile lessee continues in possession because of the law of the land, namely that the original landlord cannot physically throw out such an erstwhile tenant by force. He must get his claim for possession adjudicated by a competent Court as per the relevant provisions of law. The status of an erstwhile tenant has to be treated as a tenant at sufferance akin to a trespasser having no independent right to continue in possession.

The plaint as framed by the Plaintiff Respondent was base on a composite cause of action consisting of two parts. One part referred to the breach of the covenant on the part of the Defendant when it failed to deliver vacant possession to the Plaintiff lessor on the expiry of the lease and thereafter all throughout and thus it was guilty of breach of relevant covenants of the lease. The second part of the cause of action, however, was based on the statutory obligation of the Defendant lessee when it failed to comply with its statutory obligation Under Section 108(q) read with Section 111(a) of the Property Act. So far as this second part of the cause of action is concerned it could not certainly be said that it was arising out of the erstwhile contract.

There is no further locus poenitentiae given to the tenant to continue to remain in possession after the determination of lease by efflux of time on the basis of any such contrary express term in the lease. Consequently, it was the legal obligation flowing from Section 108(q) of the Act which would get squarely attracted on the facts of the present case and once this suit was also for enforcement of such a legal right under the law of the land available to the landlord it could not be said that enforcement of such right arose out of any of the express terms of the contract which would in turn get visited by the bar of Section 69, Sub-section (2) of the Partnership Act. Enforcement of that right had nothing to do with the earlier contract which had stood determined by efflux of time. The first point for determination, was accordingly held partly in favour of the Plaintiff and partly in favour of the Defendant. As the decree for possession was passed on the basis of both parts of causes of action, even if it was not supportable on the first part, it would remain well sustained on the second part of the very same cause of action.

• • •

CHAPTER VII

Sunil Kumar Jain Vs. Kishan and Ors., 1995

Hon'ble Judges/Coram: K. Ramaswamy and B.L. Hansaria, JJ.

Relevant Section:

Transfer Of Property Act, 1882 - Section 53-A, Delhi Lands (restrictions On Transfer) Act, 1972 - Section 4; Land Acquisition Act, 1894 [repealed] - Section 18, Section 30, Section 4, Section 4(1);

Equivalent Citation: AIR1995SC1891, 1995 (3) CCC 108 , 1995(3)SCALE682, (1995)4SCC147, [1995]3SCR855, 1995(2)UJ558, MANU/SC/0364/1995

No. of page is the original judgement: 2

Case Note:

Property - Compensation --Section 4(1)Land Acquisition Act,1894 - The Collector made an award for a sum of Rs. 38,500. Since petitioner laid claim for a higher amount - civil court disbelieved agreement of sale & High Court on an appeal said that agreement was in violation of Section 4 Delhi Land (Restriction & Transfer) Act, 1972 therefore, agreement is void - Hence, an Appeal - Whether, petitioner is entitled to compensation under Section 53-A of Transfer Property Act - Held, dispute is to title to receive compensation. It is settled law that agreement of sale does not confer title therefore, agreement holder, even assuming that agreement is valid, does not acquire any title to property & agreement is subsequent to notification under Section 4(1). - Therefore, the compensation directed to be paid to respondent since he is one of members - Appeal dismissed.

Ratio Decidendi:

" It is settled law that agreement of sale does not confer title on agreement holder"

Brief facts of the case:

Property - Agreement of sale - Section 4 of Delhi Land (Restriction & Transfer) Act, 1972 - High Court held that said agreement of sale was in violation of Section 4 of Act, and therefore, agreement was void - Accordingly, findings of Reference Court was accepted - Hence, this Petition - Whether, Respondent was undoubted owner of the property - Held, dispute was to title to receive compensation - However, it was settled law that agreement of sale did not confer title and, therefore, agreement holder, even assuming that agreement was valid, did not acquire any title to property - Thus, inter-se dispute was only with respect to title as on date of notification under Section 4(1) - Hence, Respondent was undoubted owner of property as per Section 4 notification and that, therefore, compensation was directed to be paid to respondent since he was one of the members - Thus, Court could not find any illegality in order passed by Courts

Notification under Section 4(1) of the Land Acquisition Act was published on November 17, 1980 acquiring the lands in question. The Collector made an award for a sum of Rs. 38,500. Since the petitioner laid claim for a higher amount, a reference under Section 18 was made. The civil court disbelieved the agreement of sale put forth by the petitioner; therefore, reference was ordered in favour of the respondents. In appeal, the High Court said that the said agreement was in violation of Section 4 of the Delhi Land (Restriction & Transfer) Act, 1972 and that, therefore, the agreement is void. Accordingly, the findings of the Reference Court was accepted. Thus, this appeal by Special Leave.

Held,

Learned counsel appearing for the petitioner contended that the under the agreement of sale dated 5th December, 1981 the respondents had received consideration and kept the petitioner in possession of the land and that, therefore, by operation of Section 53-A of the Transfer the Property Act, the petitioner is entitled to the compensation. We are unable to agree with the learned Counsel. In a reference, the dispute is to the title to receive the compensation. It is settled law that the agreement of sale does not confer title and, therefore, the agreement holder, even assuming that the agreement is valid, does not acquire any title to the property. It is seen that the agreement is subsequent to the notification under Section 4(1). The Government is not bound by such an agreement. The inter-se dispute is only with respect to the title as on the date of notification under Section 4(1). The Respondent is the undoubted owner of the property as per Section 4 notification and that, therefore, the compensation was directed to be paid to the respondent since he is one of the members. We cannot find any illegality in the order passed by the Courts. However, if the petitioner has got any claim under Section 30 of the Land Acquisition Act, it is open to him to take such action as open to him under law.

The Special Leave Petition is accordingly dismissed.

• • •

CHAPTER VIII

N. Srinivasa Rao Vs. Spl. Court under A.P. Land Grabbing (Prohibition) Act and Ors., 2006

Hon'ble Judges/Coram: B.P. Singh and Altamas Kabir, JJ.

Relevant Section:

Transfer Of Property Act, 1882 - Section 43, Section 6(1) Andhra Pradesh (Telangana area) tenancy and agricultural lands act, 1950 - section 47; section 49, Constitution Of India - Article 226, Article 227; Income Tax Act, 1961 - Section 2(14), Section 256(1);

Equivalent Citation: AIR2006SC3691, 2006(3)ALD10(SC), 2006(4)ALT29(SC), 2006(3)SCALE386, (2006)4SCC214, MANU/SC/8051/2006

No. of page is the original judgement: 6

Case Note:

Tenancy - land grabbing - Section 43 of Transfer of Property Act, 1882, Sections 47 and 49 of Andhra Pradesh (Telangana area) Tenancy and Agricultural Lands Act, 1950 and Andhra Pradesh land Grabbing (Prohibition) Act, 1982 - appeal against Order holding that respondent Nos. 1 to 11 were not land grabbers and further holding that Section 43 would not come to aid of transferee since transfer in absence of prior permission or sanction of tehsildar under Section 47 was prohibited - whether actions arising out of dispute raised y heirs of A can be said to attract provisions of Act of 1982 - admittedly transferees from M and C and also P have been in possession of properties and at no point had their possession been disturbed - attempts by heirs of A to dispossess said transferees could at best be said to be attempt to gain possession of lands without actually obtaining possession which would not constitute act of grabbing - in order to constitute act of land grabbing, attempt to dispossess must be followed by actual dispossession which would then constitute land grabbing so as to attract penal provisions - High Court rightly held that when initial transfer itself between A and M was invalid question of application of Section 43 to such transaction on account of subsequent acquisition of title by A would not be available - impugned Order justified.

Brief facts of the case:

One Kaneez Fatima Begum was the former owner of the lands covered by Survey No. 65 to 74 of Yousufguda village governed by the Hyderabad Tenancy and Agricultural Land Act, 1950. One Uppari Ramaiah was her tenant in respect of the said lands. From the materials on record, it appears that the said Uppari Ramaiah purchased 14 acres and 6 guntas of land from Kaneez Fatima Begum under a sale deed dated 1st May, 1961 for a consideration of Rs. 13,000/- and obtained a certificate in respect thereof under Section 38E of the Andhra Pradesh (Telangana Area) Tenancy and Agricultural Lands Act, 1950 (hereinafter referred to as the "Tenancy Act of 1950") from the Revenue Divisional Officer, Hyderabad, West. Prior to execution of the said deed, Uppari Ramaiah is purported to have sold an extent of 20,086 square yards from out of the total area measuring 14 acres and 6 guntas to one Mir Riyasat Ali by a sale deed dated 8th February, 1961. Out of the said 20,086 square yards, the said Mir Riyasat Ali sold 8,866 square yards to Smt. P. Neelakanteswaramma and to one Chandra Ramalingaiah by a sale deed dated 21st November, 1961. Their names were duly mutated in the Town Survey Registers and in the Revenue Records. On the death of Chandra Ramalingaiah on 7th February, 1973, his share in the land devolved on his legal heirs, namely, his widow, Chandra Suryamba, and his two daughters, C. Raja Kumari and P. Sandhya Kumari and son Chandra Ramakoteswar Rao. Smt. Neelakanteswaramma and the widow of Chandra Ramalingaiah entered into an agreement for sale with Bhagyalakshmi Cooperative Housing Society, but in view of the Government Order R.T. No. 3591 dated 1st December, 1975 and Government Order M.S. No. 189 dated 17th January, 1976, they could not execute the sale deeds in favour of the Housing Society.

According to P. Neelakanteswaramma and the heirs of Chandra Ramalingaiah, since the legal heirs of Uppari Ramaiah conspired to grab the lands which had been conveyed in their favour by Mir Riyasat Ali, they were constrained to file a complaint in the Special Court of A.P. Land Grabbing (Prohibition) Act, Basheerbagh, Hyderabad, being L.G.C. No. 32/1989. It was alleged in the complaint that the heirs of Uppari Ramaiah, who were made respondent Nos. 1 to 10 in the complaint, executed three General Powers of Attorney in favour of one N. Srinivasa Rao, who was made the respondent No. 11. In the said Powers of Attorney, the facts regarding transfer of the lands by Uppari Ramaiah in favour of Mir Riayasat Ali and the subsequent transfer by Mir Riyasat Ali in favour of P. Neelakanteswaramma and the predecessor-in-interest of the applicant Nos.

2 to 5 were suppressed and the property in dispute was described as the property of Uppari Ramaiah who had purchased the same from Kaneez Fatima Begum and after Uppari Ramaiah's death, it was stated that the lands had devolved on the respondent Nos. 1 to 10. as his legal heirs. By virtue of a General Power of Attorney, the said respondent Nos. 1 to 10 authorised respondent No. 11 to convert the schedule property into plots and to sell and execute sale deeds in respect thereof in favour of purchasers. The respondent Nos. 1 to 10 also executed an Agreement of Sale dated 26th June, 1980, in favour of respondent No. 11 in respect of the said lands.

Held,

In our view, in a proceeding before the Special Court the only issue which fall for decision is whether there has been an act of land grabbing as alleged and who is the guilty party. The Special Court has no jurisdiction to decide questions relating to acquisition of title by adverse possession in a proceeding under the Act as the same would fall within the domain of the civil courts. The learned Special Judge apparently traveled beyond the jurisdiction vested in him under the 1982 Act in deciding that even if the provisions of Section 47 of the Act was a bar to transfer without the sanction of the Tahsildar, the occupants of the land had perfected their title thereto by way of adverse possession.

Even on the question of the applicability of Section 43 of the Transfer of Property Act, we agree with the view taken by the High Court that when the initial transfer itself between Uppari Ramaiah and Mir Riyasat Ali was invalid, the question of application of Section 43 of the Transfer of Property Act to such a transaction on account of subsequent acquisition of title by Uppari Ramaiah would not be available.

As far as the appeals filed by N. Srinivasa Rao are concerned, his only grievance is with regard to the observations made by the Writ Court while disposing of the writ applications in his favour. Such observations appear to have been made in passing and cannot bind the parties in a properly constituted suit where the rights of the parties are to be adjudicated. We, therefore, clarify that in the event any civil action is taken by the said N. Srinivasa Rao in furtherance of his rights, if any, under the General Power of Attorney granted in his favour and/or any other document, such observations will not be relied upon in coming to a decision in the suit.

We do not think that the orders passed by the High Court call for any interference in these appeals which are disposed of accordingly. There will be no order as to costs. In our view, nothing further remains to be considered in the contempt applications and they stand disposed of accordingly.

• • •

CHAPTER IX

Suraj Lamp and Industries Pvt. Ltd. Vs. State of Haryana and Ors., 2011

Hon'ble Judges/Coram: R.V. Raveendran, A.K. Patnaik and H.L. Gokhale, JJ.

Relevant Section:

Transfer Of Property Act, 1882 - Section 53A

Equivalent Citation: 2011XAD(SC)365, 2011(107)AIC1, AIR2012SC206, 2012(1)ALLMR464, 2012(1)ALLMR(SC)464, 2011 (89) ALR 445, 2011(6)ALT1(SC), 2011(3)ARC645, 2011 (6) AWC 6296 (SC), 2012(1)BomCR293, (SCSuppl)2012(2)CHN52, [2012]169CompCas133(SC), 2011(6)CTC90, 2011(II)CLR(SC)1000, 183(2011)DLT1(SC), 2011(126)DRJ209, 2011(2)HLR545, [2012]340ITR1(SC), 2011(6)KarLJ69, 2011(4)KLJ682, 2011-5-LW289, (2011)8MLJ43(SC), 2011(4)RCR(Civil)669, 2012 115 RD1, 2011(11)SCALE438, (2012)1SCC656, [2011]11SCR848, [2011]202TAXMAN607(SC), 2011(2)U.D.609, MANU/SC/1222/2011

No. of page is the original judgement: 6

Case Note:

Property - Validity of Transaction - Section 53A of Transfer of Property Act,1882 - Four states confirmed SA/GPA/WILL transactions wherein transferred required to be discouraged as they lead to loss of revenue (stamp duty) and increase in litigations due to defective title - Hence, this Appeal - Whether, SA/GPA/WILL transactions was valid - Held, immovable property could be legally and lawfully transferred/conveyed only by registered deed of conveyance - Transactions of nature of GPA sales or SA/GPA/WILL transfers did not convey title and did not amount to transfer, nor could they be recognized or valid mode of transfer of immoveable property - SA/GPA/WILL transactions were not transfers or sales and that such transactions could not be treated as completed transfers or conveyances - They could be continue to be treated as existing agreement of sale - However, nothing prevented affected parties from getting registered Deeds of Conveyance to complete their title - SA/GPA/WILL transactions could also be used to obtain specific performance or to defend possession under Section 53A of Act - If they were entered before this day, they could be relied upon to apply for regularization of allotments/ leases by Development Authorities - It was established that if documents relating to SA/GPA/WILL transactions was accepted acted upon by DDA or other developmental authorities or by Municipal or revenue authorities to effect mutation, they need not be disturbed, merely on account of decision - Therefore, SA/GPA/WILL transactions, sale agreements and powers of attorney executed in genuine transactions and valid - Petition disposed of.

Ratio Decidendi

"Transactions of agreement shall be valid if it is treating as completed transfers or conveyances."

Brief facts of the case:

By an earlier order dated 15.5.2009 (reported in Suraj Lamp and Industries Pvt. Ltd. v. State of Haryana and Anr. MANU/SC/1021/2009 : 2009 (7) SCC 363 we had referred to the ill -effects of what is known as General Power of Attorney Sales (for short 'GPA Sales') or Sale Agreement/ General Power of Attorney/Will transfers (for short 'SA/GPA/WILL' transfers). Both the descriptions are misnomers as there cannot be a sale by execution of a power of attorney nor can there be a transfer by execution of an agreement of sale and a power of attorney and will. As noticed in the earlier order, these kinds of transactions were evolved to avoid prohibitions/conditions regarding certain transfers, to avoid payment of stamp duty and registration charges on deeds of conveyance, to avoid payment of capital gains on transfers, to invest unaccounted money ('black money') and to avoid payment of 'unearned increases' due to Development Authorities on transfer.

The modus operandi in such SA/GPA/WILL transactions is for the vendor or person claiming to be the owner to receive the agreed consideration, deliver possession of the property to the purchaser and execute the following documents or variations thereof:

(a) An Agreement of sale by the vendor in favor of the purchaser confirming the terms of sale, delivery of possession and payment of full consideration and undertaking to execute any document as and when required in future.

Or

An agreement of sale agreeing to sell the property, with a separate affidavit confirming receipt of full price and delivery of possession and undertaking to execute sale deed whenever required.

(b) An Irrevocable General Power of Attorney by the vendor in favor of the purchaser or his nominee authorizing him to manage, deal with and dispose of the property without reference to the vendor.

Or

A General Power of Attorney by the vendor in favor of the purchaser or his nominee authorizing the attorney holder to sell or transfer the property and a Special Power of Attorney to manage the property.

(c) A will bequeathing the property to the purchaser (as a safeguard against the consequences of death of the vendor before transfer is effected).

Held,

We have merely drawn attention to and reiterated the well-settled legal position that SA/GPA/WILL transactions are not 'transfers' or 'sales' and that such transactions cannot be treated as completed transfers or conveyances. They can continue to be treated as existing agreement of sale. Nothing prevents affected parties from getting registered Deeds of Conveyance to complete their title. The said 'SA/GPA/WILL transactions' may also be used to obtain specific performance or to defend possession under Section 53A of Transfer of Property Act. If they are entered before this day, they may be relied upon to apply for regularization of allotments/ leases by Development Authorities. We make it clear that if the documents relating to 'SA/GPA/WILL transactions' has been accepted acted upon by DDA or other developmental authorities or by the Municipal or revenue authorities to effect mutation, they need not be disturbed, merely on account of this decision.

We make it clear that our observations are not intended to in any way affect the validity of sale agreements and powers of attorney executed in genuine transactions. For example, a person may give a power of attorney to his spouse, son, daughter, brother, sister or a relative to manage his affairs or to execute a deed of conveyance. A person may enter into a development agreement with a land developer or builder for developing the land either by forming plots or by constructing apartment buildings and in that behalf execute an agreement of sale and grant a Power of Attorney empowering the developer to execute agreements of sale or conveyances in regard to individual plots of land or undivided shares in the land relating to apartments in favor of prospective purchasers. In several States, the execution of such development agreements and powers of attorney are already regulated by law and subjected to specific stamp duty. Our observations regarding 'SA/GPA/WILL transactions' are not intended to apply to such bonafide/genuine transactions.

We place on record our appreciation for the assistance rendered by Mr. Gopal Subramaniun, Senior Counsel, initially as Solicitor General and later as Amicus Curiae.

As the issue relating to validity of SA/GPA/WILL has been dealt with by this order, what remains is the consideration of the special leave petition on its merits. List the special leave petition for final disposal.

• • •

CHAPTER X

Harishchandra Hegde Vs. State of Karnataka and Ors., 2003

Hon'ble Judges/Coram: S.B. Sinha and Arun Kumar, JJ.

Relevant Section:

Transfer of Property Act, 1882 - Section 51, Section 51, Section 57

Equivalent Citation: 2004(15)AIC138, 2004(2)ALD75(SC), 2004 (1) CCC 224 , 2004(1)CTC709, 2004(I)CLR(SC)427, JT2005(11)SC331, 2004(1)SCALE48, (2004)9SCC780, [2003]Supp6SCR1111, MANU/SC/1113/2003

No. of page is the original judgement: 4

Case Note:

Transfer of Property Act, 1882 - Section 51 - Karnataka Scheduled Casts and Scheduled Tribes (Prohibition of Transfer of Certain lands) Act, 1978 - Sections 4,5 - Prohibition of transfer of granted lands - Resumption of granted lands - Benefit of Section 51 - Entitlement to - Grant of suit property by Government of Karnataka to grantee - Appellant purchased suit land from original grantee and made improvements thereon - On Initiation of proceedings by original grantee under Section 4, order of restoration of land passed by Assistant Commissioner under Section 5 - Challenged by appellant on granted that an order passed under Section 5 for restoration of land would be subject to right of transferee to claim value of improvements as prescribed under Section 51 of Transfer of Property Act - Appeal to Supreme Court - Dismissing Appeal, held that as Section 4 contains a non obstinate clause, said provision would be applicable not with standing anything contained in any agreement or any Act for time being in force - Since Act being a special Act and Transfer of Property Act being a general Act and Section 51 being applicable to inter vivos transfer and not to transfers made by operation of law, Section 51 will have no application and consequences contained in Section 5 would prevail.

Brief facts of the case:

he short question which fails for consideration in this appeal arising out of a judgment and order dated 16.2.1996 passed by the High Court of Karnataka in Writ Appeal No. 1045 of 1992 is as to whether Section 51 of the Transfer of Property. Act is applicable in the cases covered by Sections 4 and 5 of the Karnataka Scheduled Castes and Scheduled Tribes (Prohibition of Transfer of Certain Lands) Act 1978 (the Act for short).

2. On or about 1.5.1961, two acres of land in Survey No. 134/110 were granted by the Government of Karnataka, in favour of one Smt. Gangamma, The appellant purchased the said land from her through a registered sale deed for valuable consideration on 13.9.1.962 and allegedly invested a lot of money for improvements thereof. The Act came into force w.e.f. 1.1.1979.

3. By reason of Section 4 of the Act all the alienations made in contravention of the terms of Grant were declared as void and all such lands were resumed and restored to the original grantee in terms of Section 5 of the Act. On or about 11.9.1986, the original grantee made an application for initiation of a proceeding under Section 4 of the Act in pursuance whereof the proceeding was initiated against the appellant. An order of restoration of the land in favour of the original grantee was made by the Assistant Commissioner on 29.5.1987. The appellant preferred an appeal before the Deputy Commissioner there against which was also dismissed on 25.3.1989, The appellant thereafter filed a writ petition which was marked as Writ Petition No. 23216 of 1990 for a declaration that any order passed by the Assistant Commissioner under Section 5 of the Act for restoration of land would be subject to the right of the transferee to claim the value of the improvements as prescribed under Section 51 of the Transfer of Property Act. The said writ petition was dismissed by the learned Single Judge. The writ appeal filed by the appellant was also dismissed by reason of an order dated 16.2.1996.

Held,

"Tribal areas have their own problems. Tribals are historically weaker sections of the society. They need the protection of the laws as they are gullible and fall pray to the tactics of unscrupulous people, and are susceptible to exploitation on account of their innocence, poverty and backwardness extending over centuries. The Constitution of India and the laws made thereunder treat tribals and tribal areas separately wherever needed. The tribals need to be settled, need to be taken care of by the protective arm of the law, and be saved from falling prey to unscrupulous device so that they may prosper and by an evolutionary process join the mainstream of the society. The process would be slow, yet it has to be initiated and kept moving. The object sought to be achieved by the 1950 Act and the 1956 Regulations is to see that a member of an aboriginal tribe indefeasibly continues to own the property which he acquires and every" process known to law by which title in immovable property is extinguished in one person to vest in another person, should remain so confined in its operation in relation to tribals that the immovable property of one tribal may come to vest in another tribal but the title in immovable property vesting in any tribal must not come to vest, in a non-tribal. This is to see and ensure that non-tribals do not succeed in making in-roads amongst the tribals by acquiring property and developing roots in the habitat of tribals."

This Court further observed that the expression 'transfer' should be given a broader meaning.

Section 51 of the Transfer of Property Act applies to inter vivos transfers. It, as noticed hereinbefore, does not apply to a transfer made by operation of law. If a judicial order is passed restoring the land back to a member of Scheduled Tribes in terms of the purport and object of the statute, the provisions of the Transfer of Property Act cannot be applied in such a case. The matter is governed by a special statute. Unless there exists a provision therein, an order passed thereunder cannot be supplanted or supplemented with reference to another statute.

We are, therefore, of the opinion that. Section 51 of the Transfer of Property Act, cannot be held to have any application in the instant case. There is no merit in this appeal, which is accordingly dismissed. No costs.

• • •

CHAPTER XI

Sevoke Properties Ltd. Vs. West Bengal State Electricity Distribution Company Ltd., 2019

Hon'ble Judges/Coram: Dr. D.Y. Chandrachud and Hemant Gupta, JJ.

Relevant Section:

Transfer Of Property Act, 1882 - Section 106, Section 107, Section 111, Section 116; West Bengal Lands (Requisition and Acquisition) Act, 1948; Indian Stamp Act, 1899 - Section 35, Section 36; Registration Act, 1908 - Section 17, Section 17(1), Registration Act, 1908 - Section 49; Indian Registration Act, 1866; Indian Registration Act, 1871; Indian Registration Act, 1877; Specific Relief Act, 1877; Code of Civil Procedure (CPC) 1908 - Order 20 Rule 12

Equivalent Citation: AIR2019SC2664, 2019(4)ALD175, 2019(5)BLJ193, 2020 (3) CCC 209 , 2019(2) CHN (SC) 183, 2019(2)CWC345, (2019)4MLJ278, 2019(1)RCR(Rent)586, (2020)11SCC782, MANU/SC/0598/2019

No. of page is the original judgement: 5

Case Note:

Tenancy - Eviction - Possession - Suit for eviction was instituted before Trial judge - Trial court passed decree for vacant and peaceful possession - Preliminary decree for mesne profits was passed - Respondent filed appeal before High Court - By interim order, Division Bench of High Court directed that proceedings before trial Court for ascertainment of mesne profits shall continue, but no final decree shall be drawn up without leave of Court - Following order of High Court, valuer submitted report in regard to valuation of property - Trial Court accepted valuation - Order of trial court was challenged by Respondent before High Court - Said petition was dismissed by Single Judge - On appeal, Division Bench of High Court had set aside decree for possession and, in consequence, directed that suit instituted by Respondent shall stand dismissed - Hence, present appeal - Whether impugned order of setting aside decree for possession was suffer from infirmity.

Brief Facts of the case:

A suit for eviction was instituted before the Court of the Civil Judge. The Respondent filed its written statement. The trial court passed a decree for vacant and peaceful possession. A preliminary decree for mesne profits was passed. The Respondent filed an appeal before the High Court. By an interim order, the Division Bench of the High Court directed that proceedings before the trial Court for ascertainment of mesne profits shall continue, but no final decree shall be drawn up without the leave of the Court. The execution proceedings were stayed, subject to deposit of the arrears of rent. Following the order of the High Court, the valuer submitted a report in regard to the valuation of the property. The trial Court accepted the valuation. The order of the trial court was challenged by the Respondent before the High Court which petition was dismissed by a Single Judge. The High Court had set aside the decree for possession and, in consequence, directed that the suit instituted by the Respondent shall stand dismissed.

Held,

In terms of the provisions of Section 107 of the Transfer of Property Act, 1882 (Act) a lease of immovable property for a term exceeding one year can only be made by a registered instrument. Admittedly, in the present case, the indenture of lease had not been registered. In consequence, the contents of the indenture would be inadmissible in evidence for the purpose of determining the terms of the contract between the parties. This was the plain consequence of the provisions of Sections 17 and 49 of the Registration Act, 1908. The only purpose for which the lease could be looked at was for assessing the nature and character of the possession of the Respondent.

In the present case, there was an express admission on the part of the Defendants that they were in occupation under the lease agreement for a period of fifteen years and that the period of lease expired. Such a specific admission on the part of the Defendants was contained in the written statement. Under Section 111(a) of the Act a lease of immovable property determines by efflux of time limited thereby. Once this be the position, there could be no manner of doubt that the position of the Respondent on the expiration of the lease was of a tenant at sufferance. In the circumstances, there was no necessity of a notice for the termination of the lease under the provisions of Section 106 of Act. The Respondent having squarely admitted in its written statement that it was in occupation for a term of fifteen years, that term having expired, the lease stood determined by efflux of time. Once the lease stood determined by efflux of time, there was no necessity for a notice of termination under Section 106.

Therefore, this Court sets aside the impugned judgment and order of the High Court and restores the judgment of the trial court. In view of the pendency of the proceedings before this Court and having due regard to the interim order that was passed by the High Court during the pendency of the appeal, the Respondent should be given the liberty of assailing the judgment of Single Judge of the High Court accepting the report of the Commissioner in regard to the determination of mesne profits. This Court grants a period of three months to the Respondent to initiate appropriate proceedings in accordance with law for assailing the judgment of the Single Judge.

• • •

CHAPTER XII

Park Street Properties (Pvt.) Ltd. Vs. Dipak Kumar Singh and Ors., 2016

Hon'ble Judges/Coram: V. Gopala Gowda and Adarsh Kumar Goel, JJ.

Relevant Section:

Transfer Of Property Act, 1882 - Section 106, Section 105, Section 106, Section 107; Registration Act, 1908 - Section 17(1), Section 49

Equivalent Citation: 2016(166)AIC84, AIR2016SC4038, AIR2016SC4038, 2017(1)AJR729, 2016(5)ALD179, 2016 (119) ALR 447, 2016 (3) CCC 430 , 2016(II)CLR(SC)658, 2016(4)KLJ47, 2017(2)MhLj32, 2017(1)MPLJ550, 2016(II)OLR633, 2016(4)RCR(Civil)243, 2016(2)RCR(Rent)297, 2017 134 RD127, 2016(8)SCALE327, 2016 (8) SCJ 305, (2017)1WBLR(SC)1, MANU/SC/0960/2016

No. of page is the original judgement: 6

Case Note:

Tenancy - Termination - Clause of agreement - Validity thereof - Section 106 of Transfer of Property Act, 1882 - Trial Court decreed suit in favour of Appellant - Respondents were directed to vacate suit premises - High Court has set aside order of Trial Court - Remanded matter to it for reconsideration of validity of notice issued by Appellant terminating monthly tenancy of Respondents - Hence, present appeal - Whether agreement through which tenancy of suit premises was created in favour of Respondents, could be read in evidence - Whether it was contract to contrary in terms of Section 106 of Act.

Brief Facts of the case:

A company/owner had let out the suit premises in favour of the Appellant with the right to sublet the same or portions thereof. The Appellant entered into an agreement with the Respondents subletting the suit premises for the purpose of carrying out business from the Restaurant. Subsequently, the Respondents requested the Appellant to allow them to run franchise. In pursuance of the same, the agreement was terminated, and a tenancy of the suit premises was created in favour of the Respondents on the basis of an unregistered agreement. As per the terms of the agreement, in case of breach of the agreement, the Appellant was entitled to terminate the tenancy after serving a notice of period of thirty days. The Appellant issued a notice in question under Section 106 of the Transfer of Property Act, 1882 terminating the monthly tenancy of the Respondents in respect of the tenanted premises upon the expiry of 15 days from the date of receipt of the said notice. The Respondents did not vacate the suit premises. The Appellant filed suit. The Respondents contested the suit inter alia contending that by necessary implication the parties had agreed to not terminate the lease of the premises before 30 years, and that it was for this reason, a Clause was incorporated for enhancement of monthly rent at the rate of 15% after expiry of every 3 years. The Trial Court decreed the suit in favour of the Appellant. The Respondents were accordingly, directed to vacate the suit premises within three months from the date of the order. The High Court allowed the Respondents' appeal and remanded the suit back to the Trial Court for reconsideration from the stage of examining the question of validity of notice. Hence, the present appeal filed by the Appellant.

Held,

Section 106 of the Act makes it clear that it creates a deemed monthly tenancy in those cases where there is no express contract to the contrary, which is terminable at a notice period of 15 days.

As per Clause of the agreement, the landlord was entitled to terminate the tenancy in case there was a breach of the terms of the agreement or in case of non-payment of rent for three consecutive months and the tenants failed to remedy the same within a period of thirty days of the receipt of the notice. The said Clause of the agreement was clearly contrary to the provisions of Section 106 of the Act. While Section 106 of the Act does contain the phrase 'in the absence of a contract to the contrary', the same must be a valid contract. In the absence of registration of a document, what is deemed to be created is a month to month tenancy, the termination of which is governed by Section 106 of the Act.

The question of remanding the matter back to the Trial Court to consider it afresh in view of the fact that the same was admitted in evidence, did not arise at all. While the agreement could be admitted in evidence and even relied upon by the parties to prove the factum of the tenancy, the terms of the same could not be used to derogate from the statutory provision of Section 106 of the Act, which creates a fiction of tenancy in absence of a registered instrument creating the same. If the argument advanced on behalf of the Respondents was taken to its logical conclusion, this lease could never be terminated, save in cases of breach by the tenant. The phrase 'contract to the contrary' in Section 106 of the Act could not be read to mean that the parties are free to contract out of the express provisions of the law, thereby defeating its very intent. The impugned judgment and order passed by the High Court was set aside. The judgment and order passed by the Trial Court was restored.

• • •

CHAPTER XIII

Videocon Properties Ltd. Vs. Bhalchandra Laboratories and Ors., 2006

Hon'ble Judges/Coram: Doraiswamy Raju and Dr. Arijit Pasayat, JJ.

Relevant Section:

Transfer Of Property Act, 1882 - Section 55, Section 55, Section 55(4)(b), Section 55(6), Section 55(6)(b)

Equivalent Citation: 2004(15)AIC340, AIR2004SC1787, 2004(2)ALD87(SC), 2004(5)ALLMR(SC)559, 2004 (54) ALR 575, 2004(3)ARC88, 2004 (2) AWC 1470 (SC), 2004(106(2))BOMLR802, 2004 (1) CCC 296 , 2004(I)CLR(SC)295, JT2004(5)SC490, 2004-2-LW871, 2004(1)RCR(Civil)548, 2003(10)SCALE1085, (2004)3SCC711, [2003]Supp6SCR1197, 2004(1)UC529, 2004(1)UJ653, MANU/SC/1097/2003

No. of page is the original judgement: 6

Case Note:

Transfer of Property Act, 1882 - Section 55 (6) (b)--Rights and liabilities of buyer and seller--Scope of Section 55 (6) (b)--Appellants entering into agreement with respondents whereby landed property was to be sold by respondents--Rs. 38 lakhs paid by appellants to respondents as deposit or earnest money on execution of agreement--Nearly after five years, respondents expressing their inability to satisfy terms of agreement within time -- Appellants terminating agreement and calling upon respondents to refund Rs. 38 lakhs with 21% interest--Respondents sending cheque for Rs. 38 lakhs denying interest--Appellants filing suit in High Court--Single Judge granting temporary injunction restraining respondents from disposing of land during pendency of suit--Interpreting Section 55 (6) (b), Division Bench held single Judge in error in granting injunction--And granted interim order for depositing interest at 10% in Court--Whether Division Bench justified?--Held, "no"--Intention of parties to agreement was to treat Rs. 38 lakhs as part of pre-paid purchase money and not pure simple earnest money deposit--As sale deed not executed due to lapses and inabilities of respondents--Sum of Rs. 38 lakhs became refundable attracting first limb of Section 55 (6) (b)--And defendants/respondents prima facie became liable to refund same with interest due thereon--Order of single Judge rightly passed and restored--Order of Division Bench set aside.

The buyer's charge engrafted in Clause (b) of paragraph 6 of Section 55 of the Transfer of Property Act, 1882, would extend and enure to the purchase-money or earnest money paid before the title passes and property has been delivered by the purchaser to the seller, on the seller's interest in the property unless the purchaser has improperly declined to accept delivery of property or when he properly declines to accept delivery-including for the interest on purchase money and costs awarded to the purchaser of a suit to compel specific performance of the contract or to obtain a decree for its rescission. The principle underlying the above provision is a trite principle of justice, equity and good conscience. The charge would last until the conveyance is executed by the seller and possession is also given to the purchaser and ceases only thereafter. The charge will not be lost by merely accepting delivery of possession alone. This charge is a statutory charge in favour of a buyer and is different from contractual charge to which the buyer may become entitled to under the terms of the contract, and in substance a converse to the charge created in favour of the seller under Section 55 (4) (b). Consequently, the buyer is entitled to enforce the said charge against the property and for that purpose, trace the property even in the hands of third parties and even when the property is converted into another form, by proceeding against the substituted security, since none claiming under the seller including a third party purchaser can take advantage of any plea based even on want of notice of the charge. The said statutory charge gets attracted and attaches to the property for the benefit of the buyer the moment he pays any part of the purchase money and is only lost in case of purchaser's own default or his improper refusal to accept delivery. So far as payment of interest is concerned, the section specifically envisages payment of interest upon the purchase-money/price prepaid, though not so specifically on the earnest money deposit, apparently for the reason that an amount paid as earnest money simplicitor, as mere security for due performance does not become repayable till the contract or agreement got terminated and it is shown that the purchaser has not failed to carry out his part of the contract, and the termination was brought about not due to his fault, the claim of the purchaser for refund of earnest money deposit will not arise for being asserted.

Brief facts of the case:

The appellants are the plaintiffs in suit No. 2145 of 2000, on the original side of the High Court of Bombay and the respondents-defendants are registered firm of partnership and its partners, respectively. The plaintiffs are builders and developers and they have entered into an agreement with the defendants on 13.5.1994 to sell the landed property owned by the respondents and a sum of Rs. 38 lakhs was said to have been paid by the appellants as deposit or earnest money on the execution of the agreement, which the respondents received under the agreement. Clause 2.3 of the agreement, insofar as it is relevant for the purpose, reads as hereunder:

"If for any reason the vendors fail to fulfill their obligation under Clause 2, the purchasers shall have an option either to fulfill the said obligation themselves at the cost and expenses of the vendors or to terminate the agreement, in which event the vendors shall return to the purchasers the earnest with interest at 21% per annum..."

Clauses 17 and 18 also read as under:

"If the vendors fail to make out a marketable title to this said land agreed to be sold, as herein agreed, the purchasers snail be entitled to cancel this agreement. In the event of cancellation of this agreement under this clause, the said earnest money or deposit shall be forthwith returned to the purchasers by the vendors without any interest, cost or compensation.

If the sale be not completed due to any willful default on the part of the vendors, the purchasers shall be entitled (a) to require specific performance by the vendors of this agreement or (b) to payment by the venders of the interest at the rate of 21% per annum on the said earnest money or deposit and all costs, charges and expenses incurred and all loss and damages sustained by the purchasers in addition to the return by the vendors of the said earnest money or deposit."

Held,

Coming to the facts of the case, it is seen from the agreement dated 13.5.1994 entered into between parties - particularly Clause 1, which specifies more than one enumerated categories of payment to be made by the purchaser in the manner and at stages indicated therein, as consideration for the ultimate sale to be made and completed. The further fact that the sum of Rs. 38 lakhs had to be paid on the date of execution of the agreement itself, with the other remaining categories of sums being stipulated for payment at different and subsequent stages as well as execution of the sale deed by the Vendors taken together with the contents of the stipulation made in Clause 2.3, providing for the return of it, if for any reason the Vendors fail to fulfill their obligations under Clause 2, strongly supports and strengthens the claim of the appellants that the intention of the parties in the case on hand is in effect to treat the sum of Rs. 38 lakhs to be part of the prepaid purchase-money and not pure and simple earnest money deposit of the restricted sense and tenor, wholly unrelated to the purchase price as such in any manner. The mention made in the agreement or description of the same otherwise as "deposit or earnest money" and not merely as earnest money, inevitably leads to the inescapable conclusion that the same has to and was really meant to serve both purposes as envisaged in the decision noticed supra. In substance, it is, therefore, really a deposit or payment of advance as well and for that matter actually part payment of purchase price, only. In the teeth of the further fact situation that the sale could not be completed by execution of the sale deed in this case only due to lapses and inabilities on the part of the respondents - irrespective of bonafides or otherwise involved in such delay and lapses, the amount of rupees 33 lakhs becomes refundable by the Vendors to the purchasers as of the prepaid purchase price deposited with the Vendors. Consequently, the sum of rupees 38 lakhs to be refunded would attract the first limb or part of Section 55(6)(b) of the Transfer of Property Act itself and therefore necessarily, as held by the learned Single Judge, the defendants prima facie became liable to refund the same with interest due thereon, in terms of Clause 2.3 of the agreement Therefore, the statutory charge envisaged therein would get attracted to and encompass the whole of the sum of rupees 38 lakhs and the interest due thereon. In the light of the above, in our view, the learned Single Judge on the original side was right in passing the order dated 23.10.2001 and the order of the Division Bench, taking a contrary view in the order under challenge, is contrary to law and the reasons assigned therefore cannot be countenanced. Hence, the same is hereby set aside and the order of the learned Single Judge shall stand restored, and to be in force pending disposal of the suit.

The question relating to manner of appropriation, attempted to be argued before us, is really a matter, which has to be, properly speaking canvassed and got adjudicated in the suit only and we express no opinion on the same.

So far as the submission made that the injunction granted should not completely foreclose the liberties of the respondents, if an appropriate offer comes to sell the property after seeking directions of the judge on the original side, we leave liberties with the parties as and when necessary to approach the court before which the suit is pending for any such permission and the court after hearing the plaintiffs as well on any such request may consider the request in this regard on the defendants/respondents sufficiently securing and safeguarding the interests of the plaintiff by depositing in court to the credit of the suit so much of the sale consideration, as would be necessary to meet the claims of the plaintiffs before granting any such permission so that the amount so deposited may abide by the ultimate decision in the suit, to satisfy the decree that may be passed.

The appeal is accordingly allowed as indicated above. No costs

• • •

CHAPTER XIV

Girish Vyas and Ors. Vs. The State of Maharastra and Ors., 2011

Hon'ble Judges/Coram: R.V. Raveendran and H.L. Gokhale, JJ.

Relevant Sections:

Transfer Of Property Act, 1882 - Section 23(1), Section 37, Section 38, Section 45, Section 47, Code of Civil Procedure, 1908 (CPC) - Section 80; Section 9; Constitution Of India - Article 166, Article 21, Article 21A, Article 226, Article 243W, Article 45; Land Acquisition Act, 1894 [repealed] - Section 11, Section 11A, Section 12(2), Section 16, Section 17, Section 18, Section 23(1A), Section 23(2), Section 37(1), Section 4, Section 54, Section 5A, Section 6, Section 6(2), Section 9; Maharashtra Regional And Town Planning Act, 1966 - Section 10(2), Section 1, Section 10(1), Section 11, Section 126, Section 126(1), Section 126(1)(c), Section 126(2), Section 128, Section 129, Section 14, Section 152, Section 154, Section 16, Section 165(1), Section 165(2), Section 17, Section 2(19), Section 2(3), Section 2(9), Section 21, Section 21(1), Section 22, Section 22A, Section 26, Section 27, Section 28, Section 29, Section 3, Section 30, Section 31, Section 31(6), Section 37, Section 37(1), Section 38(A), Section 39, Section 4, Section 4(1), Section 40(3)(e), Section 42, Section 43, Section 44, Section 45, Section 46, Section 47, Section 49, Section 49(1), Section 49(4), Section 50, Section 51(2), Section 52, Section 58, Section 59, Section 59(1)(a), Section 59(1)(b), Section 59(1)(b)(i), Section 59(2), Section 6, Section 68, Section 69, Section 69(6), Section 83, Section 92; Prevention Of Corruption Act, 1988 - Section 13(1)(d)

Equivalent Citation: AIR2012SC2043, AIR2012SC2043, 2012(5)ALLMR(SC)392, JT2011(12)SC298, 2011(11)SCALE676, (2012)3SCC619, [2011]12SCR781, MANU/SC/1218/2011

No. of page is the original judgement: 42

Case Note:

Property - Cancellation of development permission - Section 165 of MR Transfer of Property Act,1966 - Division Bench passed order in respect of cancellation construction certificates - Hence, this Petition - Whether, order passed by High Court was justified - Held, Division Bench observed that, as per Principal Town Planning scheme and Development Plan framed under Section 165 of the Act, reservation on plot which was initially for play-ground had shifted for primary school - Request of landowner was to shift reservation of primary school and to grant him permission for development - On other hand, developer wanted to retain half of flats of building which was contrary to provision in Development Plan - However, direction given by State Government for deletion of reservation on Plot and commencement certificates issued by Municipal Corporation in favour of developer - Once, State Government published draft Development Plan, providing for reservation for primary school, any construction contrary thereto could not be permitted - However, on direction of Minister of State that Municipal Commissioner had given report - As provided under Act, State Government could not made order sanctioning deletion of reservation on report of Municipal Commissioner - However, personal relationship of developer with Chief Minister was used to obtain permission for construction - After all necessary directions were decided, Chief Minister placed on record his approval - Therefore, Division Bench was justified in cancelling development permission which was granted by State Government - Appeal disposed of.

Ratio Decidendi

"Order passed by authorities in respect of Cancellation of development permission over property in dispute shall be in accordance with law

Brief Facts of the case:

These appeals arise out of two writ petitions in public interest leading to concurrent judgments and a common order dated 6th - 15th March 1999 passed by a Division Bench of the Bombay High Court. These writ petitions bearing Nos. 4433 and 4434 of 1998 were filed respectively by one Vijay Krishna Kumbhar, a journalist and one Nitin Duttatraya Jagtap, a Municipal Corporator of Pune. The petitions pointed out that a particular plot of land bearing Final Plot No. 110 (F.P. No. 110 for short), and admeasuring about 3450 sq. meters, situated on Prabhat Road in the Erandwana area of the city, was initially reserved for a public purpose namely, a garden/playground, and subsequently for a primary school. They further pointed out that a number of years after the Pune Municipal Corporation (hereinafter referred to as PMC) took all the necessary steps to acquire this particular plot of land, the landowner one Dr. Laxmikant Madhav Murudkar appointed M/s Vyas Constructions, a proprietary concern of one Shri Girish Vyas (the Appellant in Civil Appeal No. 198-199 of 2000) as the developer of the property. Shri Girish Vyas is the son-in-law of Shri Manohar Joshi who was the Chief Minister of Maharashtra from 14.03.1995 till January 1999. The Petitioners contended that only because of the instructions from the Urban Development Department (UDD for short) which was under Shri Manohar Joshi, that in spite of the reservation for a primary school, the plot was permitted to be developed for private residences flouting all norms and mandatory legal provisions. They sought to challenge the building permission which was issued by the PMC under the instructions of the State Government, by submitting that these instructions amounted to interference into the lawful exercise of the powers of the Municipal Corporation, and the same was mala fide. After hearing all concerned, the petitions were allowed, and an order has been passed to cancel the Commencement (of construction) certificates, and Occupation Certificate, and to pull down the concerned building which has been constructed in the meanwhile. The State Government has been directed to initiate criminal investigation against Shri Manohar Joshi, Shri Ravindra Murlidhar Mane, the then Minister of State for UDD, and the then Pune Municipal Commissioner Shri Ram Nath Jha.

Being aggrieved by this order, the present group of appeals have been filed:

(i) Civil Appeal Nos. 198-199/ 2000 are filed by the developer Shri Girish Vyas and his proprietary concern M/s Vyas Constructions. Civil Appeal No. 2450 of 2000 is filed by the landowner Dr. Laxmikant Madhav Murudkar (since deceased) to challenge the judgments and the order in their entirety. Their submissions by and large are similar.

(ii) Civil Appeal Nos. 2102-2103 of 2000 are filed by Shri Manohar Joshi, the then Chief Minister, Civil Appeal Nos. 2105-2106 of 2000 are filed by Shri Ram Nath Jha who was the then Pune Municipal Commissioner, and Civil Appeal No. 2120 of 2000 is filed by Shri Ravindra Murlidhar Mane, the then Minister of State, UDD. These appeals seek to expunge the adverse remarks against the Appellants, and the order directing criminal investigation against them.

(iii) Civil Appeal Nos. 196-197 of 2000 are filed by Maruti Raghu Sawant and Ors. who were the tenants in this property. They contend that in the scheme prepared by the developer, they were to become owners of their tenements whereas under the original reservation, they were to be evicted.

Held,

In the circumstances we conclude and pass the following order -

(i) We hold that the direction given by the Government of Maharashtra for the deletion of reservation on Final Plot No. 110, at Prabhat Road, Pune, and the consequent Commencement and Occupation certificates issued by the Pune Municipal Corporation (PMC) in favour of the developer were in complete subversion of the statutory requirements of the MR Transfer of Property Act. The development permission was wholly illegal and unjustified.

(ii) The direction of the High Court in the impugned judgment dated 6/15.3.1999 in Writ Petition Nos. 4433 and 4434/1998 for demolition of the concerned building was fully legal and justified.

(iii) The contention of the landowner that his right of development for residential purposes on the concerned plot under the erstwhile Town Planning scheme subsisted in spite of coming into force of Development Plan reserving the plot for a primary school, is liable to be rejected.

(iv) The acquisition of the concerned plot of land was complete with the declaration under Section 126 of the MR Transfer of Property Act read with Section 6 of Land Acquisition Act and the same is valid and legal.

(v) The order passed by the High Court directing the Municipal Corporation to move for the revival of the First Appeal Stamp No. 18615 of 1994 was therefore necessary. The High Court is expected to decide the revived First Appeal at the earliest and preferably within four months hereafter in the light of the law and the directions given in this judgment.

(vi) The developer shall inform the PMC whether he is giving up the claim over the construction of the ten storied building (named 'Sundew Apartments') apart from the tenants' building in favour of PMC, failing which either the developer or the PMC shall take steps for demolition of the disputed building (Sundew Apartments) as per the time frame laid down in this judgment.

(vii) The former occupants of F.P No. 110 will continue to reside in the building constructed for the tenants on the terms stated in the judgment.

(viii) The corporation will not be required to pay any amount to the developer for the tenants' building constructed by him, nor for the ten storied building in the event he gives up his claim over it in favour of PMC.

(ix) The strictures passed by the High Court against the then Chief Minister of Maharashtra Shri Manohar Joshi and the then Minister of State Shri Ravindra Mane are maintained. The prayer to expunge these remarks is rejected. The remarks against the Municipal Commissioner are however deleted.

(x) The order directing criminal investigation and thereafter further action as warranted in law, is however deleted in view of the judgment of this Court in the case of Common Cause A Registered Society v. Union of India reported in MANU/SC/0437/1999 : 1999 (6) SCC 667

(xi) The then Chief Minister and the then Minister of State shall each pay cost of Rs. 15,000/- to each of the two Petitioners in the High Court towards these ten appeals, over and above the cost of Rs. 10,000/- awarded by the High Court in the writ petitions payable by each of them to the two writ Petitioners.

(xii) The State Government and the Planning authorities under the MR Transfer of Property Act shall hereafter scrupulously follow the directions and the suggested safeguards with respect to the spaces meant for public amenities.

All the appeals stand disposed of as above.

• • •

CHAPTER XV

Residents Welfare Association, Noida Vs. State of U.P. and Ors., 2009

Hon'ble Judges/Coram: Dr. Arijit Pasayat and Tarun Chatterjee, JJ.

Relevant Sections:

Transfer Of Property Act, 1882 - Section 105, Section 3, Section 54, Constitution Of India - Article 226; Indian Stamp Act, 1899 - Section 2, Section 2(10); Mines And Minerals (development And Regulation) Act, 1957 - Section 3; Registration Act, 1908 - Section 23, Section 52;

Equivalent Citation: 2009(4)ADJ204, 2009 (3) AWC 2580 (SC), 2009 (2) CCC 347 , 2009(1)CLR1032, 2009(I)CLR(SC)1032, JT2009(6)SC448, 2009-3-LW316, 2009(3)RCR(Civil)87, 2009(6)SCALE94, (2009)14SCC716, [2009]6SCR112, 2009(7)UJ3150, MANU/SC/0642/2009

No. of page is the original judgement: 9

Case Note:

Civil - Property Valuation--Deficiency of Stamp duty--Undervalued instrument of conveyance--Sections 47A of the Uttar Pradesh Stamp Act--Articles 23 and 63 of the Schedule to the Indian Stamp Act, 1899--New Okhla Industrial Development Area had allotted lands to several Co-operative Housing Societies by execution of lease deeds containing various restrictions on the transfer of leasehold rights--From 1984 to June 1997, Noida authorities were injuncted by the Civil Court from issuing transfer memorandums for grant of permission for transfer of leasehold rights--On 1st of July, 1997, a public notice was issued advertising that Noida authorities shall issue transfer memorandums with respect to the transfer of plots in question upon terms and conditions including payment of transfer premium--Sub-Registrar ordered that the stamp duty to be fixed on the documents should be as applicable to conveyance under Article 23 of the Schedule 1-B of the Stamp Act, on the basis of the current market value of the plot along with the constructed portion--Writ Petition challenging said Order was rejected by High Court--Hence, the present Appeal--Whether the condition precedent to pass an order under Section 47A of the Stamp Act, as amended by the State of Uttar Pradesh was present in the instant case--Whether the relevant date for determining the consideration entered in the document would be the market value of the property on the day of entering into the agreement for sale and not the date of presentation of the documents for registration--Held, the object underlying Section 47 A of the Indian Stamp Act is to neutralize the effect of under valuation of immovable property under registered instrument of sale or exchange or gift or partition or settlement--It is not enough for the authorities for the purpose of invoking Section 47 A that the consideration amount stated in the instrument of sale is less than the prevailing market value but they must be satisfied that there is an attempt of under valuation--An enquiry under Section 47 A is also not contemplated under the Act in case of an assignment by way of lease--Article 63 of Schedule 1-B of the Stamp Act, as applicable to the State of U.P., which deals with transfer of lease by way of assignment will apply to the documents in question--Consequently, registration officer does not have any jurisdiction to enquire into the market value of a property under Section 47 A , in case Article 63 applies-Moreover, the Appellant cannot be faulted for not executing deed, as they could not execute the deed because of the failure of the Noida Authorities, to execute transfer memorandum due to the orders of injunction--Consideration to be mentioned in the document would be the market value of the property on the date when the agreement was entered into and not when it was presented for registration--Therefore, there is no fraudulent intentions on the part of the Appellant to under value the property in order to evade stamp duty paid

Ratio Decidendi:

"Consideration to be mentioned in the document would be the market value of the property on the date when the agreement was entered into and not when it was presented for registration."

Brief Facts of the case:

New Okhla Industrial Development Area had allotted lands to several Co-operative Housing Societies by execution of lease deeds containing various restrictions on the transfer of leasehold rights and it was also stipulated therein that such lease deeds must be compulsorily registered with the sub-Registrar. Appellant Resident Welfare Association, Noida. had executed various agreements for transfer of leasehold rights with the co-operative societies, which were registered with the Office of the Sub-Registrar, Noida. However, from 1984 to June 1997, Noida authorities were injuncted by the Civil Court from issuing transfer memorandums for grant of permission for transfer of leasehold rights and on 1st of July, 1997, a public notice was issued advertising that Noida authorities shall issue transfer memorandums with respect to the transfer of plots in question upon terms and conditions including payment of transfer premium. Sub-Registrar ordered that the stamp duty to be fixed on the documents should be as applicable to conveyance under Article 23 of the Schedule 1-B of the Stamp Act, on the basis of the current market value of the plot along with the constructed portion. On Appeal, High Court rejected the Writ application of the Appellant. Hence, the present Appeal

Held,

A plain reading of Article 63 of the Schedule 1-B to the Stamp Act would, however, show that the stamp duty chargeable to a document is not on the market value of the property but on consideration indicated in the same.

If Article 63 of the Stamp Act is to be applied, duty shall be paid on the consideration of the amount of consideration shown in the deed itself and not on the market value of the land or the construction thereon. Therefore, it is clear from a reading of Article 63 that it would apply in case of a transfer of lease by way of an assignment and Article 23 applies In case of a conveyance by way of sale.

Article 63 in clear terms mentions that in case of an assignment, the duty that would be payable is the same duty as conveyance for a consideration equal to the amount of the consideration for the transfer. Thus it is clear that the duty is not calculated on the market value but on the amount of consideration mentioned in the deed itself.

If we refer Article 63 as applicable to the State of UP, it mentions that duty would be payable for a consideration equal to the amount of the consideration for the transfer. The legislature expressly has specified therefore that the stamp duty payable In case of an assignment would not be calculated on the market value of the property but on the consideration set forth in the deed itself.

Section 47 A would be applicable only when Article 23 is applicable. In case Article 63 applies, the registration officer does not have any jurisdiction to enquire into the market value of a property under Section 47 A of the said Act.

As is evident from the records placed before us, the Appellant could not execute the sale deed because of the failure of the Respondent No. 4, i.e. Noida Authorities, to execute transfer memorandum due to the Orders of injunction passed in pending litigations before the different Courts. Therefore, the Appellant cannot be faulted for not executing the same.

Therefore, we do not see any fraudulent intentions on the part of the Appellant to under value the property in order to evade stamp duty paid thereon. Since, the stamp duty is to be charged on the consideration mentioned in the document under Article 63 of Schedule 1-B of the Act in case of an assignment of lease, the consideration mentioned on the document was adequate in respect of the time when the agreement of the transfer by way of lease was registered.

Since Article 63 of the Act deals with stamp duty to be levied on the consideration set forth in an assignment by way of transfer of lease, and not on the market value of the property to be transferred, it can be misused and remedy would not be available under Section 47 A to determine the market value of the property.

Thus, accordingly, setting aside the Judgment of the High Court we hold that in the instant case Article 63 of Schedule 1-B of the Stamp Act, as applicable to the State of U.P., which deals with transfer of lease by way of assignment will apply to the documents in question. We also hold that the consideration to be mentioned in the document would be the market value of the property on the date when the agreement was entered into and not when it was presented for registration, considering the peculiar facts of this case.

• • •

CHAPTER XVI

Commissioner of Income Tax, Bombay and Ors. Vs. Podar Cement Pvt. Ltd. and Ors., 1997

Hon'ble Judges/Coram: K.S. Paripoornan, K. Venkataswami and B.N. Kirpal, JJ.

Relevant Section:

Transfer Of Property Act, 1882 - Section 14, Section 53A, Section 54, Section 55; Wealth tax Act, 1957 Section 2(17), Section 2(m), Code of Civil Procedure, 1908 (CPC) - Section 115; Gift-tax Act, 1958 [cease To Have Effect On Or After The 01.10.1998] - Section 2(xii); Gujarat Rents, Hotel And Lodging House Rates Control Act, 1947 - Section 29(2); Income Tax Act, 1961 - Section 154, Section 22, Section 23, Section 24, Section 25, Section 26, Section 27, Section 256(1), Section 256(2), Section 257, Section 269, Section 288, Section 56, Section 64(2), Section 69D, Section 93(2), Section 94(4)

Equivalent Citation: AIR1997SC2523, 1997(99(2))BOMLR416, (1997)141CTR(SC)67, [1997]226ITR625(SC), JT1997(5)SC529, 1997(4)SCALE271, (1997)5SCC482, [1997]Supp1SCR394, [1997]92TAXMAN541(SC), MANU/SC/0649/1997

No. of page is the original judgement: 13

Case Note:

Direct Taxation - Income from House Property - Section 22 of Income Tax Act, 1961 - Tribunal and Appellate authority held that income from flats should be assessed as income from house property under Section 22 and not as income from other sources under Section 56 of Act - High Court reversed finding of Tribunal - Hence, this Appeal - Whether, income derived by Assessee from flats was taxable under head income from other sources and not income from house property - Held, in common law owner mean a person who had got valid title legally conveyed to him after complying with requirements of law such as Transfer of Property Act, Registration Act, etc - However, in context of Section 22 of IT Act having regard to ground realities and further having regard to object of IT Act, owner was a person who was entitled to receive income from property in his own right - Therefore, Tribunal was not justified in holding that income derived by Assessee from flats was taxable under head income from other sources - Thus, Civil Appeal

No. 4165/94 dismissed and Civil Appeal No. 4549/ allowed.

Ratio Decidendi:

"There is no presumption as to a tax."

Brief facts of the case:

The respondent in Tax Reference Case Nos. 9-10/86 is a company and an assessee under the Act (hereinafter called the 'assessee'). It owns four flats bearing Nos. 231, 232, 241 and 242 in a building call as "Silver Arch" on Nepeansea Road, Bombay. The builders of the said building are M/ s. Malabar Industries Pvt. Ltd. Out of the four aforesaid flats, two were directly purchased by the respondent-company from the builders and the other two were purchased by its sister concern and subsequently by the assessee. The possession of the flats was taken after payment of consideration in full some time in August, 1973. It is common ground that all these flats have been let out to various persons. The rental income from these flats was included in the Return for the assessment years in question, namely, 1975-76 and 1976-77. It was the case of the assessee that the rental income from the flats was assessable as 'income from other sources' under Section 56 of the Act inasmuch as the assessee-company was not the 'legal owner' of the property in the flats. Such a claim was put forward before the Assessing Officer mainly on the ground that the title to the property (four flats) had not been conveyed to the Co-operative society which was formed by the purchasers of the flats and that so long as the ownership was not transferred in the name of the assessee the rental income from the flats could not be assessed as 'income from house property' (under Section 22 of the Act).

One other subsidiary question was also raised by the assessee that the rental income should be calculated on the bonafide annual value and not the actual rent received. As a matter of fact, the assessee has shown Rs. 49,800 as chargeable rent. The Income Tax Officer, however, has taken the annual letting value of those flats at Rs. 1,31,268 on the basis of rent receivable in respect of flats from an adjoining building. The Income Tax Officer also rejected the claim of the assessee that the income from the flats should be assessed under Section 56 of the Act.

Held,

The observations Supreme Court in *R.B. Jodha Mal Kuthiala's* case clearly fixes the liability on a person who receives or is entitled to receive the income from the property in his own right. In spite of this, the assessing officers of various circles instead of uniformly following the ratio laid down in this case have taken different diametrically opposite views depending upon the pronouncements of the concerned High Courts in the circles on the scope of section 22. The High Courts of Allahabad, Punjab and Haryana, Rajasthan, Calcutta and Patna have taken the view by correctly understanding the ratio laid down in *R.B. Jodha Mal Kuthiala's* case (supra) and the High Courts of Bombay, Delhi and Andhra Pradesh have taken a different view wrongly distinguishing on facts in *R.B. Jodha Mal Kuthiala's* case (supra). In *Smt. Kala Rani's* case (supra), the Punjab and Haryana High Court after referring to the judgment of this court in *R.B. Jodha Mal Kuthiala's* case (supra). Rejected the contention that the mere possession of the property in pursuance of an agreement to sell was not sufficient to burden the assessee with tax on any income under section 22. The contrary view taken by the other High Courts was mainly based on the facts that unless there is a registered deed conveying the property, the person in possession/enjoyment of the property cannot be considered as legal owner and, therefore, he cannot be called upon to pay the tax under section 22. The law laid down by this Court in *R.B. Jodha Mal Kuthiala's* case (supra), has been rightly understood by the High Courts of Punjab and Haryana, Patna, Rajasthan, etc. The requirement of registration of the sale deed in the context of section 22 is not warranted. The High Courts are sharply divided on this issue, one set of High Courts taking the view that the promoters/contractors after parting with possession on receipt of full consideration thereby enabling the `purchasers' to enjoy the fruits of the property, even though no registered document as required under section 54 of the Transfer of Property Act was executed, can be `owners' for the purpose of section 22. The other set of the High Courts had taken a contrary view holding that unless there is a registered sale document transferring the ownership as required under the Transfer of Property Act, the so-called purchasers cannot become owners for the purpose of section 22. Accordingly, hold that the views taken by the High Courts of Allahabad, Patna, Rajasthan, Punjab and Haryana are the correct views. The contrary view taken by the Delhi High Court is not correct.

• • •

CHAPTER XVII

Unitech Ltd. and Ors. Vs. Union of India (UOI) and Ors., 2015

Hon'ble Judges/Coram: Madan B. Lokur and S.A. Bobde, JJ.

Relevant Sections:

Transfer of Property Act, 1882 - Section 53A, Section 118, Income Tax Act, 1961 - Section 269UA, Section 269UA(2), Section 269UC, Section 269UD, Section 269UD(1).

Equivalent Citation: 2016(1)ABR121, 2015XII AD (S.C.) 605, (2016)285CTR(SC)162, [2016]381ITR456(SC), (2015)8MLJ249(SC), 2015(12)SCALE351, (2016)2SCC569, [2016]237TAXMAN361(SC), MANU/SC/1282/2015

No. of page is the original judgement: 6

Case Note:

Direct Taxation - Tax evasion - Appellant No. 2 holds subject land on lease - Entered into Collaboration agreement with Unitech - Land holder agreed to allow Unitech - Develop and construct commercial project on subject land - Technical and financial cost of Unitech - 78% of total constructed area - Be retained by Unitech - Remaining 22% transfer to share of Appellant No. 2 - Unitech created interest free security deposit - Agreement not to be construed as demise or assignment or conveyance of subject land - Show cause notice issued - Consideration for transaction - Too low and appears to be understated by more than 15% - To evade taxes - Appellant's objections rejected by Appropriate authority - Present appeal by Appellants - Against order of compulsory pre-emptive purchase - Under Chapter XXC of Income Tax Act, 1961 - Whether the collaboration agreement constitutes transfer of property - Whether the authority was justified in holding that the consideration for the subject property was understated and in holding that Vidarbha Engineering has transferred property to the extent of 78% to Unitech

Brief Facts of the case:

Vidarbha Engineering Industries-Appellant No. 2 (Vidarbha Engineering) holds on lease, three plots of land (subject land). Vidarbha Engineering decided to develop the subject land and entered into an agreement for the purpose with Unitech Ltd. (Unitech). The Memorandum of Understanding between them was formalized into a collaboration agreement. Under this agreement the land holder agreed to allow Unitech to develop and construct a commercial project on the subject land at the technical and financial cost of the latter. The parties to the agreement agreed, upon construction of the multi storied shopping cum commercial complex, that Unitech will retain 78% of the total constructed area and transfer 22% to the share of Vidarbha Engineering.

Unitech agreed to create an interest free security deposit of Rs. 10 lakhs. 50% of the deposit was made refundable on completion of the RCC structure and the other 50% on completion of the project. The parties were entitled to dispose of the saleable area of their share. It was specifically agreed that this agreement was not to be construed as a partnership between the parties. In particular, this agreement was not to be construed as a demise or assignment or conveyance of the subject land. It is significant to note that the agreement does not contain any clause by which Unitech, the developer, is to pay any consideration in terms of money to Vidarbha Engineering, the land holder. The only consideration apparently provided is the entitlement of Vidarbha Engineering to 22% of the constructed area in the proposed multi storied building.

Upon the submission of the statement Under Section 269UA of the Act, the Appropriate Authority issued a show cause notice stating that the consideration for the transaction appears to be too low and appears to be understated by more than 15%, having regard to the sale instance of a land in an adjoining locality. The Appellant raised several objections in reply to the show cause notice. The Appropriate authority considered the objections filed by the Appellants and rejected them by an order passed Under Section 269UD of the Income Tax Act.

This appeal is preferred by the Appellants, who suffered an order of compulsory pre-emptive purchase under Chapter XXC of the Income Tax Act, 1961 (the Act) passed by the Appropriate Authority Under Section 269UD of the Act.

Held,

In the first place, Vidarbha Engineering itself is a lessee holding the land on lease of 30 years from Nagpur Improvement Trust. It has no authority to transfer the land. Secondly, no clause in the agreement purports to transfer the subject land to Unitech. On the other hand, Clause 4.6 specifically provides that nothing in the agreement shall be construed to be a demise, assignment or a conveyance. The agreement thus creates a licence in favour of Unitech under which the latter may enter upon the land and at its own cost build on it and thereupon handover 22% of the built up area to the share of Vidarbha Engineering as consideration and retain 78% of the built up area.

It may appear at first blush that the collaboration agreement involves an exchange of property in the sense that the land holder transfers his property to the developer and the developer transfers 22% of the constructed area to the land holder but on a closer look this impression is quickly dispelled. Exchange is defined vide Section 118 of the Transfer of Property Act, 1882 as a mutual transfer of the ownership of one thing for the ownership of another. But it is not possible to construe the license created by Vidarbha Engineering in favour of Unitech as a transfer or acquisition of 22% share of the constructed building as a transfer in exchange.

As observed earlier Vidarbha Engineering is not an owner but only a lessee of the land. As such, it cannot convey a title which it does not possess itself. In fact, no clause in the agreement purports to effect a transfer. Also in consideration of the licence Unitech has agreed that the Vidarbha Engineering will have a share of 22% in the constructed area. Thus, it appears that what is contemplated is that upon construction Unitech will retain 78% and the share of Vidarbha Engineering will be 22% of the built up area vide Clause 4.6 of the agreement. Thus the transaction cannot be construed as a sale, lease or a licence.

It is clear from the agreement that the transfer of rights of Vidarbha Engineering in its land does not amount to any sale, exchange or lease of such land, since, only possessory rights have been granted to Unitech to construct the building on the land. Nor is there any clause in the agreement expressly transferring 22% of the building to Vidarbha after it is constructed by Unitech. Clause 4.6 only mentions that as a consideration for Unitech agreeing to develop the property it shall retain 78% and the share of Vidarbha Engineering will be 22%. In fact the Parliament has defined "transfer", deliberately wide enough to include within its scope such agreements or arrangements which have the effect of transferring all the important rights in land for future considerations such as part acquisition of shares in buildings to be constructed, vide Sub-clause (ii) of Clause (f) of Sub-section (2) of Section 269UA.

There is no doubt that the collaboration agreement can be construed as an agreement and in any case an arrangement which has the effect of transferring and in any case enabling the enjoyment, of such property. Undoubtedly, the collaboration agreement enables Unitech to enjoy the property of Vidarbha Engineering for the purpose of construction. There is also no doubt that an agreement is an arrangement. It must therefore be held that the collaboration agreement effectuates a transfer of the subject land from Vidarbha Engineering to Unitech within the meaning of the term in Section 269UA of the Act. It appears to be the intention of the Parliament to cover all such transactions by which valuable rights in property are in fact transferred by one party to another for consideration, under the word "transfer", for fulfilling the purpose of pre-emptive purchase i.e. prevention of tax evasion

Moreover, as rightly contended, the authorities have treated the consideration for subject land, which is an industrial plot, as understated by more than 15% on the basis of a sale instance of a land which is in a residential locality. More importantly, it is obvious that the area of the sale instance is of a much smaller plot whereas the subject land which is said to have been undervalued is larger. It is well known that the price of a small residential plot would be more than a large industrial plot. The show cause notice which has subsequently been confirmed is vitiated by a gross non-application of mind.

The authority fell into a gross and an obvious error while conducting this entire exercise of holding that the consideration for the subject property was understated in holding that Vidarbha Engineering has transferred property to the extent of 78% to Unitech. There is no warrant for this finding since Vidarbha Engineering was never to be the owner of the entire built up area. It only had a share of 22% in it. Unitech, which had built from its own funds, was to retain 78% share in the built up area. And in any case the Appellants had never stated that the consideration for Rs. 1,00,40,000/- was in respect of the built up area but on the other hand had clearly stated that it was for transfer of the subject land. Thus, there was no evidence on record nor is any referred to in the order for coming to the conclusion that Vidarbha Engineering had transferred 78% of the built up area to Unitech and retained 22%. The order of appropriate authority thus suffers from a gross perversity.

Undoubtedly one of the objects of the provision is to prevent evasion of taxes by showing an undervaluation which is more than 15% of the true value of the property and which in turn carries an implication that some portion of the value is not shown in the agreement or the deed but passes by way of unaccounted money. But it is not possible to say that it must be alleged in the show cause notice or a finding must be rendered in the order that there is evasion of taxes as a sine qua non for its validity. Nor is it possible to hold that the onus of establishing undervaluation with a view to evade tax is on the revenue. The true position seems to be that a significant undervaluation, greater than 15% below the fair market value raises a rebuttable presumption that there is an attempt to evade taxes.

The High Court has failed to render a finding on the relevance of comparable sale instances, particularly, why a sale instance in an adjoining locality has been considered to be valid instead of a sale instance in the same locality. The other aspects of the impugned order of the appropriate authority in the earlier part of judgment seems to have been missed.

• • •

CHAPTER XVIII

Trustees of Sahebzadi Oalia Kulsum Trust and Ors. Vs. The Controller of Estate Duty A.P., 1998

Hon'ble Judges/Coram: S.V. Manohar and M. Srinivasan, JJ.

Relevant Section:

Transfer Of Property Act, 1882 - Section 13; Section 14, Section 2, Section 13, Section 14, Section 2

Equivalent Citation: 1996 (1) AWC 799 (SC), 1998 (3) CCC 77 , (1998)148CTR(SC)391, MANU/SC/2133/1998

No. of page is the original judgement: 4

Case Note:

Trusts and Societies - Validity of Trusts - Estate Duty - Sections 13 and 14 of Transfer of Property Act, 1882 - Whether both trusts are valid and liable for purposes of estate duty ? - Held, considering principles of Mohammedan Law, two trusts created in relevant year are valid wakfs - Wakif-settlor made dedication in perpetuity of subject matter of these trusts for purposes which are considered pious under Islamic Law - Therefore properties ceased to be properties of settlor on creation of wakfs in relevant year - When settlor died, they could not form part of his estate settlor having divested himself of these properties fourteen years prior to his death - Therefore beneficial interest created in favour of daughter in law is valid creation of trust which is not affected by Sections 13 and 14 of Act - As result settlor had divested himself of these properties during his lifetime for benefit of his grand daughter and thereafter for their descendants - On date of his death settler did not have any interest in properties nor had he reserved any interest to himself under these trusts - Therefore for purposes of duty, deceased cannot be considered as having any interest in trust property which passed on his death - Therefore properties which constituted two trusts cannot be included in estate of deceased for purposes ot duty - Hence, impugned order set aside and appeals allowed

Brief facts of the case:

On 21-3-1953, the Nizam of Hyderabad, Sir Mir Osman Ali Khan executed a deed of trust under which he settled certain jewellery and other properties on trust for the benefit of Sahebzadi Oalia Kulsum, his grand daughter for life and thereafter for her children and their children for life etc. and ultimately for the maintenance of a holy shrine. On the same date, he also executed a deed of trust in favour of his daughter-in-law, Sahebzadi Anwar Begum, the wife of second Prince Muazzam Jah. The terms of the two trust deeds are similar. For the sake of convenience, we are referring only to the trust deed executed in favour of Sahebzadi Oalia Kulsum.

Under the deed of trust, the settlor who was a Muslim, created a trust in respect of certain jewellery and ornaments and other properties for the benefit of his grand daughter Oalia Kulsum who was given a right to wear the jewellery after her marriage or on completing the age of 30 years whichever was earlier. She was allowed to wear the jewellery and ornaments during her life time and after her death the trustees were directed to sell the ornaments and invest the sale proceeds, thus turning them into an income yielding investment. A further direction was given to the trustees to pay the income to the children of Oalia Kulsum or remoter issue of Prince Muazzam Jah Bahadur from generation to generation in the ratio of two shares for male and one share female heirs. In the absence of the contingencies mentioned above, the income was directed to be paid to remoter issues of Prince Muazzam Jah Bahadur from generation to generation in the ratio of two shares for male and one share for female. On the death of the last survivor of the persons entitled to the net income of the fund, the income was directed to be utilised for the benefit of the holy shrine at Khum in Iran. Thus the trust was in the nature of a wakf-alal-aulad. In fact the recital in trust deed is to the same effect.

Held,

Although the High Court referred, *inter alia* to the Privy Council decision in *Abul Fata Mohammad Ishak* (supra) and the Mussalman Wakf Validation Acts 1913 and 1930 which applied only to British India, it appears to have accepted the submission that the court was obliged to apply the original principles of Mohammedan Law in as much as H.E.H. the Nizam in the Charter granted to the High Court directed that in cases when the parties were Muslims the case would be governed by Sharai-Shariff. The High Court held the wakf to be invalid under Mohammaden Law.

Of course, in the case before it, both under the law as declared by the Privy Council as also the dictum of Imam Mohammed (said to be no different from that of Abu Yusuf on this issue) the wakf was invalid. But the High Court, in the light of its Charter also took the assistance of Mohammedan Law as laid down by Islamic authorities in deciding the issue.

In the light of the principles of Mohammedan Law as set out earlier, the two trusts created in 1953 in the present case are valid wakfs. The wakif-settlor made a dedication in perpetuity of the subject matter of these trusts for purposes which are considered pious under Islamic Law. The properties, therefore, ceased to be the properties of the settlor on the creation of the wakfs in 1953. When the settlor died in 1967, they could not form a part of his estate the settlor having divested himself of these properties fourteen years prior to his death.

The appellant has also pointed out that during the life time of the settlor, the income-tax authorities had accepted the validity of the wakfs and had not treated the income of the wakfs as the income of the settlor

In the present case, therefore, the beneficial interest created in favour of Oalia Kulsum and Anwar Begum is a valid creation of trust which is not affected by sections 13 and 14 of the Transfer of Property Act. As a result the settlor had divested himself of these properties during his lifetime for the benefit of his grand daughter Oalia Kulsum and his daughter-in-law Anwar Begum and thereafter for their descendants and then for the holy shrine at Khum. On the date of his death the settler did not have any interest in the properties nor had he reserved any interest to himself under these trusts. Hence, for the purposes of Estate Duty, the deceased cannot be considered as having any interest in the trust property which passed on his death. The properties which constituted the subject matter of the two trusts, therefore, cannot be included in the estate of the deceased Sir Mir Osman Ali Khan, the Nizam of Hyderabad for the purposes of estate duty.

In the premises, the judgment and order of the High Court are set aside and the two questions are answered in the negative and in favour of the appellant. The appeals are accordingly allowed with costs

• • •

CHAPTER XIX

Commissioner of Income Tax, Jaipur vs. Sirehmal Nawalakha, 2001

Hon'ble Judges/Coram: B.N. Kirpal and Shivaraj V. Patil, JJ.

Relevant Sections:

Transfer Of Property Act, 1882 - Section 122, Section 123, Gift-tax Act, 1958 [cease To Have Effect On Or After The 01.10.1998] - Section 2(xii), Section 4; Registration Act, 1908 - Section 17

Equivalent Citation: 2001VIIAD(SC)464, AIR2001SC3648, 2001 (45) ALR 149, 2001 (3) CCC 231 , (2001)169CTR(SC)493, [2001]251ITR108(SC), JT2001(7)SC69, 2001(5)SCALE394, (2001)6SCC641, [2001]118TAXMAN316(SC), 2001(2)UC366, MANU/SC/0469/2001

No. of page is the original judgement: 3

Case Note:

Direct Taxation - registered document - Sections 122 and 123 of Transfer of Property Act, 1882 and Sections 2 and 4 of Gift Tax Act, 1958 - whether appellant can claim assessment on unregistered gift under Act of 1958 - document not registered legally not valid - High Court held that on unregistered documents appellant not liable for assessment - High Court in error holding that appellant not liable for assessment - order passed by High Court set-aside - appeal allowed.

Brief facts of the case:

The respondent was the owner of immovable property and by declaration dated 10th October, 1966 he sought to give a gift of certain out-houses attached to a building to his wife.

The declaration which was made not registered. The Gift Tax Officer rejected the respondent's claim that a valid gift has been made as, according to him, there had not been any compliance with the provisions of Section 123 of the Transfer of Property Act. The Assistant Commissioner and the Tribunal took the same view and thereafter following question of law was referred to the High Court by the Tribunal :

"Whatever on the facts and circumstances of the case, the Tribunal was justified in law in holding that no valid gift of out-houses of the building named as "Deep Shikha" was made by the assessee to his wife in terms of the Gift-tax Act, 1958?"

Held,

The respondent seeks to bring its case within the provisions of clause (c) or (d) of Section 4. There can be no doubt in our mind that surrender or forfeiture of an interest in immovable property as contemplated by clause (c) of Section 4 or vesting of any property in another person as contemplated by clause (d) of Section 4 in the case of an immovable property would attract the provisions of Section 17 of the Registration Act. What is important in that there has to be a valid transfer of property and whether that transfer amounts to a gift or not would bring in to question the applicability of the provisions of the Gift Tax Act.

As we have already observed, there may be certain transactions of transfer which may not amount to a gift within the meaning of Section 122 of the Transfer of Property Act but would be regarded as gifts for the purpose of subjecting such transfers to the levy of gift tax. In this behalf, reference may usefully be made to Commissioner or Gift Tax, Kerala vs. R Valsala Amma MANU/SC/0251/1971 : [1971]82ITR828(SC) wherein this Court at page 830 observed that "the Gift-tax Act did not change the general law relating to the rights of property". The general law would take into its ambit not only the provisions of the Transfer of Property Act but would also require application of the provisions of the Registration Act. It is not necessary for us to refer to the decisions of the High Courts in this behalf except to note that the consistent view of the High Courts has been that for effecting a transfer the provisions of the Transfer of Property Act and/or the Registration Act have to be complied with. (See Smt. Padma Lalchand Mirchandani vs. Commissioner of Income Tax, New Delhi MANU/DE/0146/1979 : [1981]128ITR174(Delhi) ; Commissioner of Gift-tax, Bombay III vs. Matilda Ferreira MANU/MH/0093/1977 : [1978]112ITR934(Bom) ; K.Madhavakrishnan vs. Commissioner of Gift-tax, Tamil Nadu MANU/TN/0438/1979 : [1980]124ITR233(Mad) and Darbar Shivrajkumar vs. Commissioner of Gift-tax, Gujarat-IV MANU/GJ/0082/1981 : [1981]131ITR647(Guj).

In the instant case, the High Court did not even refer to the provisions of the Registration Act and, therefore, fell in error in coming to the conclusion that the case fell within the provisions of Section 4 of the Gift Tax Act and, therefore, as it was a deemed gift it was not necessary that the document has to be registered. In our view, the general law did not stand abrogated and the requirement of complying with the provisions of the Transfer of

Property Act and the Registration Act had to be fulfilled. The High Court, therefore, erred in answering the question of law in the negative and against the Revenue.

For the aforesaid reasons, this appeal is allowed, the judgment of the High Court is set aside and the question of law in answered in favour of the appellant. No costs.

• • •

CHAPTER XX

Commissioner of Income Tax, Hyderabad Vs. Motors and General Stores (P.) Ltd., 1967

Hon'ble Judges/Coram: J.C. Shah, S.M. Sikri and Vaidynathier Ramaswami, JJ.

Relevant Section:

Transfer Of Property Act, 1882 - Section 118; Section 54; Sale Of Goods Act, 1930 - Section 2

Equivalent Citation: AIR1968SC200, 1968(1)AnWR26, [1967]66ITR692(SC), (1968)IMLJ26, [1967]3SCR876, MANU/SC/0100/1967

No. of page is the original judgement: 4

Case Note:

Direct Taxation - assessment - Sections 54 and 118 of Transfer of Property Act - appeal by special leave on behalf of Commissioner from judgment of High Court - respondent is private limited company owning cinema house - taxed on profits made by exhibition of films - question of law decided by High Court was whether transaction dated 21.02.1956 amounts to sale within Income Tax Act - High Court answered question in favour of assessee company - Apex Court observed that name given to transaction by parties concerned does not necessarily decide nature of transaction - transaction which would escape tax is not taxable on ground that same result could be brought about by a transaction in another form which would attract tax - Apex Court held, question rightly answered by High Court in favour of assessee company.

Brief facts of the case:

his appeal is brought, by special leave, on behalf of the Commissioner of Income-tax, Hyderabad from the judgment of the Andhra Pradesh High Court dated October 30, 1964 in case Referred No. 6 of 1963.

2. The respondent (hereinafter referred to as the 'assessee-company') is a private limited company owning a cinema house called "Sree Rama Talkies", at Bobbili. It was being taxed on the profits made by exhibition of films therein. At a meeting of its Board of Directors held on September 9, 1955, it was resolved that the managing director, the Raja of Bobbili may be authorised to negotiate with the Zamindar of Chikkavaram or his

nominee for the sale of the entire concern with all its equipment and machinery, fittings, etc. for a consideration of Rs. 1,20,000/-. An agreement was concluded to effect a sale and this was confirmed by the assessee-company at an extra-ordinary general body meeting on October 4, 1955. Pursuant thereto, a deed called the "exchange deed" was brought into existence on February 21, 1956 and the consideration was received by the assessee-company in the shape of transfer of 5% tax-free cumulative preference shares in Sri Rama Sugar and Industries Ltd., Bobbili, of the face value of Rs. 1,20,000/-held by the Zamindar and Zamindarini of Chikkavaram. Separate valuation was given for the immovable property and for the movables etc., and good will, each being valued at Rs. 60,000/-. For the assessment year 1956-57, the assessee-company submitted a return of income showing a sum of Rs. 9,823/-as profits derived from the transaction. The Income-tax Officer found that the value realised exceeded the written down value by Rs. 43,568/- and accordingly computed the profits under section 10(2)(vii) of the Income-tax Act, 1922 and included the amount in the taxable income of the assessee-company. The order of the Income-tax Officer was confirmed by the Appellate Assistant Commissioner in appeal and by the Income-tax Appellate Tribunal except for allowing a sum of Rs. 5,000/-as representing the cost of goodwill. As directed by the High Court, the Appellate Tribunal stated a case under section 66(2) of the Income-tax Act, 1922 on the following question of law

" (1) Whether the transaction dated 21-2-1956 amounts to a sale within the purview of the second proviso to section 10(2) (vii) of the Indian Income-tax Act; alternatively,

(2) Whether, the consideration for the sale is not the market value of the shares as on the date of transaction, namely, Rs. 95/-per share, but the face value of the shares."

Held,

In a later case - Commissioners of Inland Revenue v. Wesleyan and General Assurance Society 30 T.C. 11, Viscount Simon expressed the principle as follows :

"It may be well to repeat two propositions which are well established in the application of the law relating to Income Tax. First, the name given to a transaction by the parties concerned does not necessarily decide the nature of the transaction. To call a payment a loan if it is really an annuity does not assist the tax-payer, any more than to call an item a capital payment would prevent it from being regarded as an income payment if that is its true nature. The question always is what is the real character of the payment, not what the parties call it.

Secondly, a transaction which, on its true construction, is of a kind that would escape tax, is not taxable on the ground that the same result could be brought about by a transaction in another form which would attract tax."

For the reason already given we hold that the question has been rightly answered by the High Court in the negative and in favour of the assessee-company and this appeal must be dismissed with costs.

Appeal dismissed.

• • •

CHAPTER XXI

Commissioner of Income Tax, Kanpur Vs. R.S. Gupta, 1987

Hon'ble Judges/Coram: S. Natarajan and Sabyasachi Mukherjee, JJ.

Relevant Section:

Transfer Of Property Act, 1882 -Section 122, Section 123, Estate Duty Act, 1953 [repealed] - Section 10; Sale Of Goods Act, 1930 - Section 33, Section 123; Wealth-tax Act, 1957 - Section 27(1), Section 29(1)

Equivalent Citation: AIR1987SC785, (1987)60CTR(SC)115, [1987]165ITR36(SC), JT1987(1)SC340, 1987(1)SCALE225, (1987)2SCC84, [1987]2SCR121, [1987]30TAXMAN546(SC), 1987(1)UJ459, MANU/SC/0356/1987

No. of page is the original judgement: 5

Case Note:

Direct Taxation - gift - Sections 122 and 123 of Transfer of Property Act, 1882 - whether gifts made by assessee are valid - in order to constitute valid gift there must be any existing property of which gifts are to be made - mere account entries shall not constitute valid gift - in case of banking companies or other firms having overdraft facilities even if sum in reality is not available with them on date of gift their gift shall be valid - in case of other concerns this kind of gift will not be valid gift - in case at hand gift entries in books cannot constitute valid gift because business of concern is not banking business.

Brief facts of the case:

The appeal under Section 29(1) of the Wealth-tax Act, 1957 (hereinafter called the Act) is directed against the judgment and order of the High Court of Allahabad dated 6th of January 1971. The questions involved before the Allahabad High Court in the reference under Section 27(1) of the Act were as follows:

(1) Whether, on the facts and in the circumstances of the case, the Tribunal rightly held that the assessee did not make valid gifts aggregating Rs. 1,50,000 on 1.1.1957?

(2) Whether, on the facts and in the circumstances of the case, the Tribunal rightly held that the assessee did not validly assign Rs. 1,50,000 in favour of his sons and grand sons by his letter dated 1.1.1957?

(3) Whether, on the facts and in the circumstances of the case, the Tribunal rightly held that the sum of Rs. 1,50,000 was properly included in the assessee's net wealth?

(4) Whether, on the facts and in the circumstances of the case, the Tribunal rightly held that the assessee did not make valid gifts aggregating Rs. 67,560/12/-?

(5) Whether, on the facts and in the circumstances of the case, the Tribunal rightly held that the sum of Rs. 67,560/12/- was rightly included in the net wealth of the assessee?

Held,

The Court in Controller of Estate Duty, Punjab, Haryana, J. & K., H.P., and Chandigarh v. Kamlavati, MANU/SC/0318/1979 : [1979]120ITR456(SC) had to deal with gift by way of transfer in the account books. There this Court held that when the property was gifted by a donor the possession and enjoyment of which was allowed to a partnership firm in which the donor was a partner, then the mere fact of the donor sharing the enjoyment or the benefit in the property was not sufficient for the application of Section 10 of the Estate Duty Act, 1953, until and unless such enjoyment or benefit was clearly referable to the gift, i.e. to the parting with such enjoyment or benefit by the donee or permitting the donor to share them out of the bundle or rights gifted in the property. If the possession, enjoyment or benefit of the donor in the property was consistent with the facts and circumstances of the case other than those of the factum of gift, it could not be said that the donee had not retained the possession and enjoyment of the property to the entire exclusion of the donor, or, to the entire exclusion of the donor in any benefit to him by contract or otherwise. There, M, the deceased, was a partner in a firm having a half-share in the partnership. On 27th March, 1957, M made a gift of Rs. 1 lakh to his son, L, and of Rs. 50,000 to his wife, K, by making debit entries in his account in the firm and corresponding credits to the accounts of L and K. With effect from 28th March, 1957, L was taken as a partner in the firm by giving L one-forth share out of the half-share of M. M died on 9th January, 1962. The Tribunal held that Section 10 of the Estate Duty Act was not attracted and the sum of Rs. 1,50,000 could not be included in the property passing on the death of M; and the High Court, on a reference, affirmed the views of the Tribunal. This Court held affirming the decision of the High Court that Section 10 did not apply to the gifts of Rs. 1 lakh and Rs. 50,000 made by the deceased to his son and to his wife respectively. But in that case, the question in the present form in which it arises before us in the instant case did not arise.

This Court in the case of Badri Prasad Jagan Prasad v. Commissioner of Income-Tax, U.P., MANU/SC/0155/1985 : [1985]156ITR430(SC) (judgment by one of us) had occasion to refer to the effect of book entries but this question which is present before us in the present appeal was not before this Court in that case. No useful purpose, therefore, will be served by reference to that case.

In that view of the matter, except to the extent indicated above, the entries in the books of account could not effectuate gifts. As we have discussed the facts on the principles, we are of the opinion that the High Court was in error in answering the question in the manner it did. The order and judgment of the High Court are therefore set aside. All the questions are answered in favour of the revenue. As the respondent is not appearing, there will be no order as to costs.

• • •

Videos & Tv Shows On Law & Exim

List of some important videos & TV shows on Law & EXIM by Adv. Jayprakash Somani on his YouTube Channel 'Jayprakash Somani EXIM & Legal'

Legal Videos: Hindi -English

1) SLP in Supreme Court / Special Leave Petitions in the Supreme Court of India

2) Transfer of Civil & Criminal Cases by the Supreme Court of India / Transfer of Matrimonial Cases

3) Appellate Jurisdiction of the Supreme Court of India

4) Jurisdictions of the Supreme Court of India

5) Public Interest Litigation in the Supreme Court of India / PIL in Supreme Court

6) Article 32 Writ Petitions in the Supreme Court of India

7) Bail Matters Top 10 Supreme Court Cases

8) FIR Quashing in High Court & Supreme Court

9) Bail & Anticipatory Bail Matters in Supreme Court

10) Insolvency & Bankruptcy Matters in the Supreme Court

11) Insolvency & Bankruptcy Code 2016 Part 1

12) Insolvency & Bankruptcy Code 2016 Part 2

13) Insolvency & Bankruptcy Code 2016 Part 3

14) Corporate Liquidation Process

15) Supreme Court Rules & Procedures Webinar of 2.5 hour on Zoom

16) RDDBFI Act, 1993 (Introduction)

17) The Indian Contact Act 1872

18) Negotiable Instruments Act (Introduction)

19) How to avoid matrimonial disputes& some more videos

20)SEBI Matters in the Supreme Court

21) Matrimonial Matters: Supreme Court's 20 Case Laws

22) Consumer Matters Supreme Court's 20 Case Laws

23) Service Matters Supreme Court's 20 Case Laws

24) How to Search Lawyer for Your Matter

25) Property Matters Supreme Court's 20 Case Laws

26) Bail Matters: Supreme Court's 20 Case Laws

27) Supreme Court / High Court Vacation Benches

28)69000 Teacher's Recruitment Matters of UP Government in the Supreme Court

29) Contempt of Court Matters in the Supreme Court

30) Advocate Act's Matters in the Supreme Court

31) Business Law Matters in the Supreme Court

32) Banking Matters in the Supreme Court

33) Labour Law Matters in the Supreme Court

34) Arbitration Matters in the Supreme Court

35) Careers in Law -Zoom Webinar by Adv. Jayprakash Somani

36) Civil Matters in the Supreme Court

37) Consumer Protection Act | Consumer Matters in the Supreme Court

38) Corporate Matters in the Supreme Court

39) Criminal Matters in the Supreme Court

40) Role of Respondent in the Supreme Court of India

41) Motor Vehicle Accident Matters in Supreme Court with case laws

42) Article 131 Original Suits in Supreme Court

43)PIL in Supreme Court/ Public Interest Litigations in the Supreme Court of India'

44)CAB Citizenship Amendment Bill is not Unconstitutional

45) Supreme Court of India Cases & Process – Marathi

46) Legal Services Export / Export of Legal Services

47) Transfer of Matrimonial Cases by the Supreme Court of India

48) Public Interest Litigation PIL

49) The Specific Relief Act (Introduction)

50) Corporate Insolvency Resolution Process CIRP

51)ABMM's Career 5 - Careers in Law

52) Transfer of cases by Supreme Court

53) Writ Petitions in High Court & Supreme Court of India

54) Supreme Court Jurisdictions - Appeals, SLP, Writ Petitions, Transfer, Original, Review, Curative

55)LEGAL INDIA TV Show: Cases Handled in Supreme Court

56) Corporate Liquidation Process

57) Legal Services Export / Export of Legal Services

• • •

EXIM Videos: Hindi -English

1) Yes, I can do Import Export Business Easily! 36 points excellent video in Hindi

2) Yes, I can do Import Export Business Easily! 36 points excellent video in English

3) Import Export Business – Hindi video

4) Import Export Business - English video

5) Export Import Marathi TV Interview

6) Scope for Commerce Students in International Business- TV Show

7) Scope for Management Student in International Business- TV Show

8) Scope for Engineering Students in International Business – TV Show

9) Women in International Business- TV Show

10) How to do Import Export Business Successfully!‘

11) Where one can get full information on Import Export Business?

12) What to do import & export?

13) Import Export Workshop/ Training/Course/ Diploma

14) How to Start Import Export Business & How to grow it. Live Webinar

15) Success Stories & Failure Stories in Import & Export Business

16) For MSME Scope in Export & Import...

17) Exports In Agri. & Food Products – English & some more videos

18) Exports to Dubai, Aabudhabii. e. UAE

19) Jewellery Exports from India

20) How to attend EXIM workshop to become excellent Exporter

21) Import Export Best Training Course – Online & Offline

22) Agri Product Export

23) Scope for Woman in International Business

24) Management Graduates Scope in International Business

25) Pharma Product’s Export

26) Best Import Export Course | Practical Training | Aaronica Global Exim

27) Import Export Business for Commerce Graduates

28) How Do I Get Export Orders? Finding International Buyers

29) What Is APEDA In Import Export Business?

30) Which Is The Best Product To Export From India?

31)EXIM Remark by Manoj Kumar Faridabad

32)EXIM Remarks by Mahesh Telangana

33) What Licenses I Need To Start Import/ Export?

34) How Can I Increase My Import Export Business?

35) Which Is Best B2B Website For Import/Export Business?

36) Export Import Management with Global Marketing

37) How to Start Export Import Business | 51 Points Video

38) Scope for Commerce & Other Graduates in International Business

39)BE A SUCCESSFUL EXPORTER FOR OUR NATION - Marathi video

40) Export of Textile , Cotton, Agri., Food, & other products & services

41) Exports from MP, CG, MH, GJ & CA in Fresh Fruits & Vegetables

42) Exports in Agri. & Food Products- Hindi

43) Start your Online/E-Commerce Business

44) How to Start Export Import Business & Grow it

45) Exports in Textile & Other Products

46) Start and grow EXIM business - Live English Webinar

47)'Import Export Business!' Why, Who, What & How can one do it easily!!

48) Live: Export of Product & Services During & After Lock Down Period

49) Frauds in Import Export Business

50) Import Export for Business Man

51) Import & Export for Women

51) Import & Export for Graduate & Post - Graduate Students

52) Agriculture Exports from India

53) Digital Marketing Setup - Marathi

54)2nd Secret of Successful Businessman

55) Digital Marketing Set up

56) Legal Services Export / Export of Legal Services

57) Export & Import with UAE

58) Service Exports / Exports by Service Providers

59) Import Export Workshop/ Training/Course/ Diploma

60) Exports & Imports with USA

61) Selection on Product for Export

62) Top Products Exported from India

63) What to do import & export?

64)ABMM Career 2 - 'Careers in Business & Industries

65) How to do Import Export Business Successfully!'

66)5 Secrets of Successful Businessman

67) Export from MP, Chhattisgarh & Vidarbha Nagpur

68)EXIM Hindi - Textile & Apparel Export

69)EXIM Hindi - Export Import Practical Training In Delhi, Kolkata, Mumbai and Pune

70) Import Export Business

71) Import Export Business Hindi

72) Import Export Business English video

73) Import Export Business Marathi

74) Women in International Business by Exim Guru Adv. Jayprakash Somani

75) Opportunities in Foreign Trade- Adv. Jayprakash Somani's special interview

• • •

List Of Adv. Jayprakash Somani's Books

1. Supreme Court of India's Leading Case Laws on 'Insolvency & Bankruptcy Code 2016'
2. Bail Matters – Supreme Court's Latest Leading Case Laws
3. Arbitration Matters- Supreme Court's Latest Leading Case Laws
4. Property Matters - Supreme Court's Latest Leading Case Laws
5. Matrimonial Matters- Supreme Court's Latest Leading Case Laws
6. Election Matters- Supreme Court's Latest Leading Case Laws
7. SEBI Matters- Supreme Court's Latest Leading Case Laws
8. Banking Matters- Supreme Court's Latest Leading Case Laws
9. Service Matters- Supreme Court's Latest Leading Case Laws
10. Contempt of Court Matters- Supreme Court's Latest Leading Case Laws
11. Consumer Protection Matters- Supreme Court's Latest Leading Case Laws
12. Corporate Law- Supreme Court's Latest Leading Case Laws
13. Supreme Court's AOR Exam- Leading Cases
14. Armed Force Tribunal - Supreme Court's Latest Leading Case Laws
15. Acquittal From 376 - Supreme Court's Latest Leading Case Laws
16. Negotiable instrument – Supreme Court's Latest Leading Case Laws
17. Contract Act- Supreme Court's Latest Leading Case Laws
18. Insider trading- Supreme Court's Latest Leading Case Laws
19. Foreign Exchange and Management Act- Supreme Court's Latest Leading Case Laws
20. Income Tax Act- Supreme Court's Latest Leading Case Laws
21. Company Law- Supreme Court's Latest Leading Case Laws
22. Competition & Monopoly Matters- Supreme Court's Latest Leading Case Laws
23. Compassionate Appointment- Service Matters- Supreme Court's Latest Leading Case Laws
24. Compulsory Retirement- Service Matters- Supreme Court's Latest Leading Case Laws
25. Voluntary Retirement- Service Matters- Supreme Court's Latest Leading Case Laws

26. Removal/Dismissal/Termination from Service- Supreme Court's Latest Leading Case Laws

27. Seniority- Service Matter- Supreme Court's Latest Leading Case Laws

28. Promotion- Service Matter- Supreme Court's Latest Leading Case Laws

29. Equal Pay for Equal Work- Service Matter- Supreme Court's Latest Leading Case Laws

30. Condition of Service- Service Matter- Supreme Court's Latest Leading Case Laws

31. Customs Act- Supreme Court's Leading Case Laws

32. Information Technology Act- Supreme Court's Latest Leading Case Laws

33. PROFESSIONAL ETHICS OF ADVOCATES- AOR EXAM- Supreme Court's Latest Leading Case Laws

34. TRANSFER OF PROPERTY ACT - Supreme Court's Latest Leading Case Laws

• • •

These Books are available online at

1. **Notion Press:** https://notionpress.com/author/jayprakash_somani
2. **Amazon:** https://www.amazon.in/s?k=jayprakash+somani
3. **Flipkart:** https://www.flipkart.com/search?q=Jayprakash%20Somani

• • •

9 798886 410457

Printed by Libri Plureos GmbH in Hamburg,
Germany